Lecture Notes in Computer Science   10182

Commenced Publication in 1973
Founding and Former Series Editors:
Gerhard Goos, Juris Hartmanis, and Jan van Leeuwen

More information about this series at http://www.springer.com/series/7412

Jianhua Yao · Tomaž Vrtovec
Guoyan Zheng · Alejandro Frangi
Ben Glocker · Shuo Li (Eds.)

Computational Methods
and Clinical Applications
for Spine Imaging

4th International Workshop and Challenge, CSI 2016
Held in Conjunction with MICCAI 2016
Athens, Greece, October 17, 2016
Revised Selected Papers

 Springer

Editors
Jianhua Yao
National Institutes of Health
Bethesda, MA
USA

Tomaž Vrtovec
University of Ljubljana
Ljubljana
Slovenia

Guoyan Zheng
University of Bern
Bern
Switzerland

Alejandro Frangi
University of Sheffield
Sheffield
UK

Ben Glocker
Imperial College London
London
UK

Shuo Li
University of Western Ontario
London, ON
Canada

ISSN 0302-9743   ISSN 1611-3349   (electronic)
Lecture Notes in Computer Science
ISBN 978-3-319-55049-7   ISBN 978-3-319-55050-3   (eBook)
DOI 10.1007/978-3-319-55050-3

Library of Congress Control Number: 2017933559

LNCS Sublibrary: SL6 – Image Processing, Computer Vision, Pattern Recognition, and Graphics

Printed on acid-free paper

This Springer imprint is published by Springer Nature
The registered company is Springer International Publishing AG
The registered company address is: Gewerbestrasse 11, 6330 Cham, Switzerland

Preface

The spine represents both a vital central axis for the musculoskeletal system and a flexible protective shell surrounding the most important neural pathway in the body, the spinal cord. Spine-related diseases or conditions are common and cause a huge burden of morbidity and cost to society. Examples include degenerative disc disease, spinal stenosis, scoliosis, osteoporosis, herniated disks, fracture/ligamentous injury, infection, tumor, and spondyloarthropathy. Treatment varies with the disease entity, and the clinical scenario can be nonspecific. As a result, imaging is often required to help make the diagnosis. Frequently obtained studies include plain radiographs, dual-energy X-ray absorptiometry (DXA), bone scans, computed tomography (CT), magnetic resonance (MR), ultrasound, and nuclear medicine. Computational methods play a steadily increasing role in improving speed, confidence, and accuracy in reaching a final diagnosis. Although there has been great progress in the development of computational methods for spine imaging over recent years, there are a number of significant challenges in both methodology and clinical applications.

The goal of this workshop on "Computational Methods and Clinical Applications for Spine Imaging" was to bring together clinicians, computer scientists, and industrial vendors in the field of spine imaging, for reviewing state-of-art techniques, sharing novel and emerging analysis and visualization techniques, and discussing clinical challenges and open problems in this rapidly growing field. We invited papers on all major aspects of problems related to spine imaging, including clinical applications of spine imaging, computer-aided diagnosis of spine conditions, computer-aided detection of spine-related diseases, emerging computational imaging techniques for spinal diseases, fast 3D reconstruction of the spine, feature extraction, multiscale analysis, pattern recognition, image enhancement of spine imaging, image-guided spine intervention and treatment, multimodal image registration and fusion for spine imaging, novel visualization techniques, segmentation techniques for spine imaging, statistical and geometric modelling for spine and vertebra, spine and vertebra localization.

This was the fourth MICCAI workshop on Computational Methods and Clinical Applications for Spine Imaging — MICCAI–CSI2016[1], which was held on October 17, 2016, in Athens, Greece, as a satellite event of the 19th International Conference on Medical Image Computing and Computer-Assisted Intervention — MICCAI 2016. We received many high-quality submissions addressing many of the aforementioned issues. All papers underwent a thorough double-blinded review with each paper being reviewed by three members of the paper reviewing committee. The Program Committee consisted of researchers who had actively contributed to the field of spine imaging in the past. From all submissions, we finally accepted 13 papers. The papers were grouped into three sessions: Segmentation (4), Localization (5), and Computer-Aided Diagnosis and Intervention (4).

---

[1] http://csi2016.wordpress.com.

In order to give deeper insights into the field and stimulate further ideas, we had invited lectures during the workshop. We are very thankful to Dr. Tim Cootes from the University of Manchester, UK, for giving a talk on "Systems for Locating Vertebral Fractures in X-Ray Images," and Dr. Franjo Pernuš from the University of Ljubljana, Slovenia, for a talk on "Image-Guided Spine Intervention."

Finally, we would like to thank everyone who contributed to this joint workshop and challenge: the authors for their contributions; the members of the program and scientific review committee for their review work, promotion of the workshop, and general support; the invited speakers for sharing their expertise and knowledge; and the MICCAI society for the general support. The event was supported by the SpineWeb[2] initiative, a collaborative platform for research on spine imaging and image analysis, and sincere gratitude goes to Brainlab AG, Germany,[3] for the financial support.

February 2017

Jianhua Yao
Tomaž Vrtovec
Guoyan Zheng
Alejandro Frangi
Ben Glocker
Shuo Li

---

[2] http://spineweb.digitalimaginggroup.ca.

[3] http://www.brainlab.com.

Organization

Workshop Organizing Committee

Jianhua Yao	National Institutes of Health, USA
Tomaž Vrtovec	University of Ljubljana, Slovenia
Guoyan Zheng	University of Bern, Switzerland
Alejandro Frangi	University of Sheffield, UK
Ben Glocker	Imperial College London, UK
Shuo Li	University of Western Ontario, Canada

Program Committee

Ulas Bagci	University of Central Florida, USA
Paul Bromiley	University of Manchester, UK
Yunliang Cai	Dartmouth College, USA
Ananda Chowdhury	Jadavpur University, India
Daniel Forsberg	Sectra and Linköping University, Sweden
Ben Glocker	Imperial College London, UK
Huiguang He	Institute of Automation Chinese Academy of Sciences, China
Jianfei Liu	National Institutes of Health, USA
Cristian Lorenz	Philips Research, Germany
Simon Pezold	University of Basel, Switzerland
Greg Slabaugh	City University London, UK
Sovira Tan	National Institutes of Health, USA
Tamas Ungi	Queen's University, Canada
Jianhua Yao	National Institutes of Health, USA
Yiqiang Zhan	Siemens Medical Solutions, USA
Guoyan Zheng	University of Bern, Switzerland
Yuanjie Zheng	Shandong Normal University, China

Proceedings Editors

Jianhua Yao	National Institutes of Health, USA, jyao@cc.nih.gov
Tomaž Vrtovec	University of Ljubljana, Slovenia, tomaz.vrtovec@fe.uni-lj.si
Guoyan Zheng	University of Bern, Switzerland, guoyan.zheng@istb.unibe.ch
Alejandro Frangi	University of Sheffield, UK, a.frangi@sheffield.ac.uk
Ben Glocker	Imperial College London, UK, b.glocker@imperial.ac.uk
Shuo Li	University of Western Ontario, Canada, slishuo@gmail.com

Contents

Computer Aided Diagnosis and Intervention

Segmentation

Improving an Active Shape Model with Random Classification Forest for Segmentation of Cervical Vertebrae

S.M. Masudur Rahman Al Arif[1]([✉]), Michael Gundry[2],
Karen Knapp[2], and Greg Slabaugh[1]

[1] Department of Computer Science, City, University of London, London, UK
S.Al-Arif@city.ac.uk
[2] University of Exeter Medical School, Exeter, UK

Abstract. X-ray is a common modality for diagnosing cervical vertebrae injuries. Many injuries are missed by emergency physicians which later causes life threatening complications. Computer aided analysis of X-ray images has the potential to detect missed injuries. Segmentation of the vertebrae is a crucial step towards automatic injury detection system. Active shape model (ASM) is one of the most successful and popular method for vertebrae segmentation. In this work, we propose a new ASM search method based on random classification forest and a kernel density estimation-based prediction technique. The proposed method have been tested on a dataset of 90 emergency room X-ray images containing 450 vertebrae and outperformed the classical Mahalanobis distance-based ASM search and also the regression forest-based method.

Keywords: ASM · Classification forest · Cervical · Vertebrae · X-ray

1 Introduction

The cervical spine or the neck region is vulnerable to high-impact accidents like road collisions, sports mishaps and falls. Cervical radiographs is usually the first choice for emergency physicians to diagnose cervical spine injuries due to the required scanning time, cost, and the position of the spine in the human body. However, about 20% of cervical vertebrae related injuries remain undetected by emergency physicians and roughly 67% of these missing injuries result in tragic consequences, neurological deteriorations and even death [1,2]. Computer aided diagnosis of cervical X-ray images has a great potential to help the emergency physicians to detect miss-able injuries and thus reducing the risk of missing injury related consequences.

Segmentation of the cervical vertebra in X-ray images is a major part of any computer aided injury detection system. Due to the clinical importance of vertebrae segmentation, there is a large body of research in the literature [3–11]. Based on this literature, arguably the most successful segmentation method is the statistical shape model (SSM). Active shape model (ASM) is one version of the SSMs

© Springer International Publishing AG 2016
J. Yao et al. (Eds.): CSI 2016, LNCS 10182, pp. 3–15, 2016.
DOI: 10.1007/978-3-319-55050-3_1

that has been performing with success in various fields including medical and facial images. Since its inception, the algorithm has been studied and modified by many researchers [12–16]. In [12], a simple gradient maxima search has been introduced for this task. However, this method is limited to edge like object boundaries. An improved Mahalanobis distance-based search method has been introduced in [13]. This method involves a training phase and an optimization step to find the amount of displacement needed to converge the mean shape on the actual object boundary. The method has been shown to work well on cervical vertebra X-ray images in [3,4]. In [15], a conventional binary classifier and a boosted regression predictor has been compared and used to improve the performance of ASM segmentation during image search phase. While these methods detect the displacement of the shape towards the possible local minima, [16] have proposed a method to directly predict some of the shape parameters using a classification method. In the state-of-the-art work on vertebra segmentation [17], a random regression forest has used to predict the displacement during image search of constrained local model (CLM), another version of SSM.

In this paper, we propose a one-shot random classification forest-based displacement predictor for ASM segmentation of cervical vertebrae. Unlike the Mahalanobis distance-based method used in [3,4,13,14], this method predicts the displacement directly without a need of a sliding window-based search technique. Our method uses a multi-class forest in contrast with the binary classification method used in [15]. A kernel density estimation (KDE)-based classification label prediction method has been introduced which performed better than traditional classification label prediction method. The proposed algorithm has been tested on a dataset of 90 emergency room X-ray images and achieved 16.2% lower error than the Mahalanobis distance-based method and 3.3% lower fit-failure compared with a regression-based framework.

2   Methodology

Active shape model (ASM) has been used in many vertebrae segmentation frameworks. In this work, we have proposed an improvement in the image search phase of ASM segmentation using a one-shot multi-class random classification forest algorithm. The proposed method is compared with a Mahalanobis distance-based method and a random regression forest-based method. The ASM is briefly described in Sect. 2.1, followed by the Mahalanobis distance-based search method in Sect. 2.3, regression forest-based search method in Sect. 2.4 and finally the proposed search method is explained in Sect. 2.5.

2.1   Active Shape Model

Let $\mathbf{x}_i$, a vector of length $2n$ describing n 2D points of the i-th registered training vertebra, is given by:

$$\boldsymbol{x}_i = [x_{i1}, y_{i1}, x_{i2}, y_{i2}, x_{i3}, y_{i3}, ..., x_{in}, y_{in}] \tag{1}$$

where (x_{ij}, y_{ij}) is the Cartesian coordinate of the j-th point of the i-th training vertebra. A mean shape, $\bar{\mathbf{x}}$, can be calculated by averaging all the shapes:

$$\bar{x} = \frac{1}{N} \sum_{i=1}^{N} x_i \qquad (2)$$

where N is the number of vertebrae available in the training set. Now, the covariance, Λ, is given by

$$\Lambda = \frac{1}{N-1} \sum_{i=1}^{N} (x_i - \bar{x})(x_i - \bar{x})^T \qquad (3)$$

Principal component analysis (PCA) is performed by calculating $2n$ eigenvectors p_k $(k = 1, 2, ..., 2n)$ of Λ. The eigenvectors with smaller eigenvalues (λ_k) are often result from noise and/or high frequency variation. Thus any shape, x_i, can be approximated fairly accurately only by considering first m eigenvectors with largest eigenvalues.

$$\hat{x}_i \approx \bar{x} + P_s b_i; \qquad P_s = [p_1, p_2, ..., p_m] \qquad (4)$$

where b_i is a set of weights known as shape parameters. The standard practice to select m is to find the first few eigenvalues, λ_k's, that represent a certain percentage of the total variance of the training data. For any known shape, x_i, shape parameter b_i can be computed as:

$$b_i = P_s^T (x_i - \bar{x}) \qquad (5)$$

2.2   ASM Search

When segmenting a vertebra in a new image, the mean shape is approximately initialized near the vertebra using manually clicked vertebra centers [18, 19].

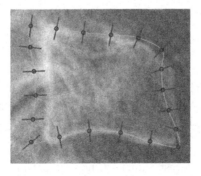

Fig. 1. ASM search: extraction of normal profiles. Initialized mean shape (magenta), extracted profiles (green) and shape describing points (blue). (Color figure online)

The model then looks for displacement of the mean shape towards the actual vertebra based on the extracted profiles perpendicular to the mean shape in the image (see Fig. 1). In [12], a simple gradient maxima search have been introduced for this task but however this method is limited to edge like object boundaries. An improved Mahalanobis distance-based search method has been introduced in [13]. This method has been used for vertebrae segmentation in [3,4].

2.3   Mahalanobis Distance-Based ASM Search (ASM-M)

The Mahalanobis distance-based ASM search involves a training phase and an optimization step to find the amount of displacement needed to converge the mean shape on actual object boundary. During training for each landmark point, intensity profiles of length $2l+1$ are collected from all the objects. The normalized first derivatives these profiles (g) are then used to create a mean profile $(\bar{g})$ and a covariance matrix (Λ_g). When a new profile, g_k, is given, then the Mahalanobis distance can be calculated as:

$$M(g_k) = (g_k - \bar{g})\Lambda_g^{-1}(g_k - \bar{g}) \tag{6}$$

The profile g_k is then shifted from the mean shape inwards and outwards by l pixels and Mahalanobis distance is computed at each position. The desired amount of displacement $(\hat{k})$ is then computed by minimizing $M(g_k)$, which is equivalent to maximizing the probability that g_k originates from a multidimensional Gaussian distribution learned from the training data. The one-dimensional displacements $(\hat{k})$ for all the points are then mapped into 2D displacement vector dx. This dx reconfigures the mean shape towards the actual object boundary.

$$db = P_s^T dx; \qquad b_t = b_{t-1} + db; \qquad \hat{x}_t = \hat{x}_{t-1} + P_s b_t \tag{7}$$

where $\hat{x}_0 = \bar{x}$ and b_0 is an all zero vector. The process is iterative. The reconfiguration stops if number of iterations, t, crosses a maximum threshold or dx is negligible.

2.4   Random Regression Forest-Based ASM Search (ASM-RRF)

Regression-based method has been used for ASM search in [15]. Random forest (RF) is a powerful machine learning algorithm [20]. It can be applied to achieve classification and/or regression [21]. Recent state-of-the-art work on vertebrae segmentation [17], proposed a random forest regression voting (RFRV) method for this purpose in the CLM framework. The regressor predicts a 2D displacement for the shape to move towards a local minimum. In order to compare the performance of our proposed one-shot multi-class random classification forest-based ASM search, a random regression forest-based ASM search has also been implemented. This forest trains on the gradient profiles collected during a training phase and predicts a 1D displacement during ASM search.

ASM-RRF Training: The ASM-M produces a displacement $\hat{k}$ by minimizing Eq. 6 over a range of displacements. The predicted displacement $(\hat{k})$ can take any value from $-l$ to $+l$ representing the amount of shift needed. The ASM-RRF is also designed to produce the same, only by looking at the gradient profile $(\boldsymbol{g})$. To achieve this, the profile vectors $(\boldsymbol{g})$ for each landmark point are collected based on the manual segmentation curves of the object. The profiles with manually segmented annotations at the center pixel are assigned shift label 0, then the profile extraction window is shifted inwards or outwards to create positive and negative shift labels representing the position of the manually annotated segmentation pixel with respect to the center. To make the process equivalent to the previous ASM-M method, the amount of shifting was limited to $\pm l$ pixels, giving us a total of $2l + 1$ regression target values to train the forest. The forest is trained using standard information gain and regression entropy i.e. variance of the target values.

$$IG = H(S) - \sum_{i \epsilon \{L,R\}} \frac{|S^l|}{S} H(S^i) \tag{8}$$

$$H(S) = H_{reg}(S) = Var(L_S) \tag{9}$$

where S is a set of examples arriving at a node and S^L, S^R are the data that travel left or right respectively and L_S is the set of target value available at the node considered. In our case, $L_S \subset \{-l, -l + 1, ..., 0, ..., l - 1, l\}$. The node splitting stops when the tree reaches a maximum depth (D_{max}) or number of elements at node falls below a threshold $(nMin)$. The leaf node records the statistics of the node elements by saving the mean displacement, $\bar{k}_{ln}$ and the standard deviation $\sigma_{k_{ln}}$ of the node target values.

ASM-RRF Prediction: At test time new profiles are fed into the forest and they regress down to the leaf nodes of different trees. A number of voting strategies for regression framework are compared in [17]: a single vote at $\bar{k}_{ln}$, a probabilistic voting weighted by $\sigma_{k_{ln}}$ or a Gaussian spread of votes $N(\bar{k}_{ln}, \sigma_{k_{ln}})$. They reported the best performance using the single vote method. Following this, in this paper, the displacement $\hat{k}$ is determined by Eq. 10. This $\hat{k}$ is then returned to the ASM search process to reconfigure the shape for next iteration.

$$\hat{k} = \frac{1}{T} \sum_{t=1}^{T} (\bar{k}_{ln_t}) \tag{10}$$

where T is the number of trees in the forest.

2.5   Random Classification Forest-Based ASM Search (ASM-RCF)

The main contribution of this work is to provide an alternative to the already proposed ASM-M and ASM-RRF methods with the help of random classification forest (ASM-RCF) algorithm. Classification-based ASM search methods have previously been investigated in [15,16]. A binary classification-based method is proposed in [15] to predict the displacement while [16] proposed another classification-based to determine first few shape parameters directly. Like [15] our also ASM-RCF method determines the displacement but instead of a binary classification, the problem is designed as a multi-class classification problem. Thus like regression, it can predict the displacement in one-shot without the need of sliding window search like ASM-M method and [15].

ASM-RCF Training: The training data is the same as the ASM-RRF method. Gradient profiles (g) are collected using manual segmentations and shifted inwards and outwards to create $2l + 1$ shift labels. But, instead of considering the shift labels as continuous regression target values, here we consider them as discrete classification labels. The classification forest is then trained to predict $2l + 1$ class labels. The same information gain of Eq. 8 is used but the entropy $H(S)$ is replaced by the classification entropy of Eq. 11.

$$H(S) = H_{class}(S) = -\sum_{c \epsilon C} p(c) log(p(c)) \tag{11}$$

where C is the set of classes available at the node considered. Here, $C \subset \{-l, -l+1, ..., 0, ..., l-1, l\}$. Both ASM-RRF and ASM-RCF are parametrized by maximum depth (D_{max}), minimum node element ($nMin$), number of trees (T), numbers of random variables ($nVar$) and numbers of random threshold values ($nThresh$) to considers for node optimization.

ASM-RCF Prediction: The leaf nodes of our classification forest are associated with a set of labels, $C_{ln_{xy}}$, that contains all the target classification labels present at that leaf node.

$$C_{ln_{xy}} = \{c_1, c_2, ..., c_{n_{Leaf_{xy}}}\} \tag{12}$$

where $n_{Leaf_{xy}}$ is the number of elements at the x-th leaf node of y-th tree of the forest. At test time, a new profile is fed into the forest and it reaches different leaf nodes of different trees. We have experimented with two different prediction methods. First, a classical *ArgMax* based classification label predictors and other is a Gaussian kernel-based classification label predictor.

ArgMax based label prediction (RCF-AM): The set of leaf node labels from each tree is collected in C_{forest}. The collection of labels is then converted into a probabilistic distribution over the $2l + 1$ classification labels as $p(C_{forest})$. Finally, the predicted label $\hat{c}$ (or the displacement $\hat{k}$) is determined by finding the label that maximizes $p(C_{forest})$.

$$\hat{k} = \hat{c}_{argmax} = \arg\max_c p(C_{forest}) \tag{13}$$

where

$$C_{forest} = \{C_{tree_1} \cup C_{tree_2} \cup .... \cup C_{tree_T}\} \tag{14}$$

$$C_{tree_y} = C_{ln_{xy}} = \{c_1, c_2, ..., c_{n_{Leaf_{xy}}}\} \tag{15}$$

Kernel based label prediction (RCF-KDE): Apart from the RCF-AM method, we propose a new kernel density estimator (KDE) based method to determine the classification label $\hat{c}$ or the displacement $\hat{k}$ of the test profile. KDE-based predictors are most commonly used in regression forests. But here, we demonstrate its usefulness as a multi-class label predictor for classification forest. Like RCF-AM, here we also collect the all the leaf node labels as C_{forest}. Then at each element c_{in} of C_{forest} a zero mean Gaussian distribution with variance σ^2_{kde} is added. The predicted class $\hat{c}$ is determined by the label that maximizes the resultant distribution.

$$\hat{k} = \hat{c} = \arg\max_c \left(\frac{1}{s} \sum_{i=1}^{s} \left(\frac{1}{\sigma_{kde}\sqrt{2\pi}} \exp^{-\frac{(x-c_{in_i})^2}{2\sigma^2_{kde}}} \right) \right) \tag{16}$$

where s is number of class labels in C_{forest}. Figure 2 shows an toy example of different prediction methods for a forest with a single tree.

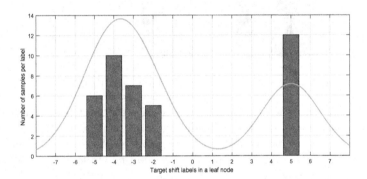

Fig. 2. An example leaf node and different prediction methods: In this particular leaf node there are in total 40 samples: the shift labels are -5, -4, -3, -2 and 4; number of samples per label are 6, 10, 7, 5 and 12 respectively. The regression mean of ASM-RRF method for this leaf node is zero, class label prediction with ArgMax (ASM-RCF-AM) method is label 5 and with ASM-RCF-KDE method is label -4. The magenta curve represents the summed kernel densities. (Color figure online)

3 Experiments

3.1 Data

A total of 90 X-ray images have been used for this work. Different (Philips, Agfa, Kodak, GE) radiographic systems were used for the scans. Pixel spacing varied from 0.1 to 0.194 pixel per millimetre. The dataset is very challenging and

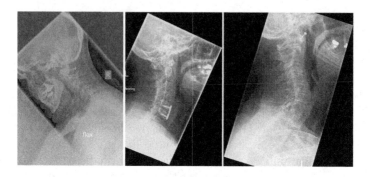

Fig. 3. Example of images in the dataset.

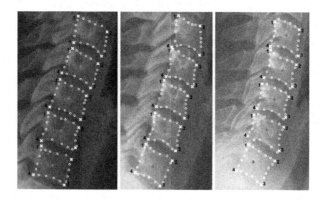

Fig. 4. Manual segmentations: centers $(+)$, corners ( ) and other points ( ).

contains natural variations, deformations, injuries and implants. A few images from the dataset are shown in Fig. 3. Each of these images was then manually demarcated by expert radiographers. Radiographers clicked on 20 points along the vertebra boundary. Some manual demarcation points for C3–C7 are shown in Fig. 4. The axis (C1) and atlas (C2) of the cervical vertebrae have not been studied in this work due to their ambiguity in lateral X-ray images similar to other work in the literature [3,4].

3.2 Training

An ASM is trained for each vertebra separately. Five models are created for five vertebrae. The means and covariance matrices for ASM-M are computed separately for each landmark point of each vertebra. The forests (ASM-RRF and ASM-RCF) are trained separately for each side of the vertebrae (anterior, posterior, superior and inferior). To increase the forest training samples, the 20 point segmentation shape is converted into a 200 point shape using Catmull-Rom spline. The training profiles are collected from these points. The training profiles for all ASM search methods are of length 27 i.e. $l = 13$, giving us a total of 27 shift labels: $\{-13, -12, ..., 0, ..., 12, 13\}$.

3.3   Segmentation Evaluation

A 10-fold cross-validation scheme has been followed. For each fold, the ASM, ASM-M, ASM-RRF and ASM-RCF training has been done on 81 images and tested on 9 images. After training, each fold consists of 5 vertebrae ASM models (mean shape, Eigen vectors and Eigen values), (5 vertebra $\times$ 20 points =) 100 mean gradient profiles and covariance matrices for ASM-M method and (5 $\times$ 4 sides =) 20 forests each for ASM-RRF and ASM-RCF methods. Each forest is trained on (200 points $\times$ 27 labels $\times$ 81 training images $\div$ 4 sides =) 109350 samples. The experiment is repeated 10 times so that each image in our dataset of 90 images are considered as test image once. At the end of the experiments, the Euclidean distance between predicted vertebra shape points and manual segmentation curves are computed in millimetres as the error metric. The distance errors are calculated for each segmentation point and averaged over all the vertebrae as a single metric.

3.4   Parameter Optimization

There are five free parameters in the random forest training: the number of trees (T), maximum allowed depth of a tree (D_{max}), minimum number of elements at a node ($nMin$), number of variables to look at in each split nodes ($nVar$) and number of thresholds ($nTresh$) to consider per variable. Apart from these, the kernel density estimation function requires a bandwidth (BW) which is the variance σ^2_{kde} of Eq. 16. A greedy sequential approach is employed to optimize each parameter due to time constraint. The sequence followed is: BW, T, D and $nMin$ in a 2D fashion, and $nVar$ and $nThresh$ in a 2D fashion. The cost function for the optimization is the average absolute difference between predicted and actual class labels. Figure 5 shows an example parameter search for BW. BW is chosen based on the minimum error found on the graph i.e. 1.5. Similarly, all the parameters are optimized and reported in Table 1.

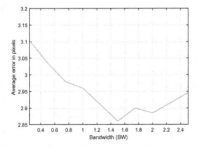

Fig. 5. Bandwidth optimization.

Table 1. Optimized parameters.

Parameters	Value
BW	1.5
T	100
D_{max}	10
$nMin$	50
$nVar$	6
$nThresh$	5

4   Results

The mean, median and standard deviation of the average errors in millime-
ters have been reported in Table 2. Both random forest-based methods perform
better than the ASM-M method. Among two options of ASM-RCF methods,
KDE method outperforms the ArgMax (AM) method. ASM-RCF-KDE shows
an improvement of 16.1% in terms of median error over ASM-M method. ASM-
RCF-KDE also outperforms regression-based ASM-RRF slightly in terms of
mean and median. The algorithms are also compared using fit-failures. In this
work, fit-failure is defined as the percentage vertebra having an average error of
1 mm or higher. The last row of Table 2 report the fit-failures. In terms of this
metric, both classification (ASM-RCF) based methods outperform other methods and ASM-RCF-KDE performs the best with the lowest failure rate of 16.67%.
The algorithms are also compared in Fig. 6 where the proportion of the vertebrae
is shown as a cumulative distribution function over the errors. More area under
the curve indicates better performance. It can be seen that ASM-RCF-KDE
and ASM-RRF are the two best algorithms for ASM search. The cropped and
zoomed version, Fig. 6 (right), indicates that our proposed method ASM-RCF-
KDE slightly outperforms the current state-of-the-art regression-based method.
Some qualitative segmentation results for ASM-RCF-KDE method with the
manual segmentation has been shown in Fig. 7. The method successfully segments most of the vertebrae. The performance is satisfactory for the vertebrae
with low contrast (4a) and implants (5a) too. But the algorithm still requires
future work. Row (b) of Fig. 7 shows challenging segmentation cases where the

Table 2. Performance comparison: average error in MM.

	ASM-M	ASM-RRF	ASM-RCF-AM	ASM-RCF-KDE
Median	0.8019	0.6933	0.7054	**0.6896**
Mean	0.8582	0.7704	0.8060	**0.7688**
Standard deviation	**0.3437**	0.3766	0.3998	0.3965
Fit failures (%Errors >1 mm)	24.00	21.78	20.00	**16.67**

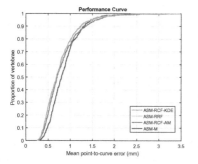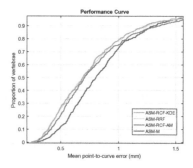

Fig. 6. Comparison of performance.

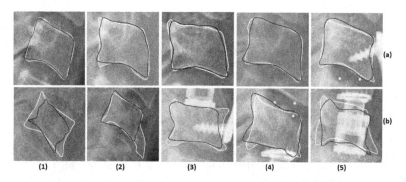

Fig. 7. Segmentation results: manual segmentation (green), ASM-RCF-KDE (blue). (Color figure online)

segmentation was unsuccessful. It can be seen that the segmentation sometimes suffers from low contrast and bad initialization (1b), deformity (2b) and implants (3b, 4b and 5b).

5   Conclusion

In this paper, we have provided an alternative to standard active shape model algorithm by introducing a one-shot multi-class random forest in the ASM search process. The new algorithm has been formulated as a classification problem which eliminates the sliding window search of Mahalanobis distances-based method. The improved algorithm provides better segmentation results and an improvement of 16.1% in point to line segmentation errors has been achieved for a challenging dataset over ASM-M. The proposed classification forest-based framework with kernel density-based prediction (ASM-RCF-KDE) outperformed regression-based methods by 3.3% in terms of fit-failures. The proposed KDE-based prediction helps to predict the displacement with better accuracy because it can nullify the effect of false tree predictions by using information from neighbouring classes (Fig. 2).

Our algorithm has been tested on a challenging dataset of 90 emergency room X-ray images containing 450 cervical vertebrae. We have achieved a lowest average error of 0.7688 mm. In comparison, current state-of-the-art work [17], reports an average error of 0.59 mm for a different dataset of DXA images on healthy thoraco-lumbar spine. Their method uses the latest version of SSM, constrained local model (CLM) with random forest regression voting based search method. In the near future, we plan to work on CLM with a classification forest-based search method. As our overarching goal is to develop an injury detection system, the segmentation still requires further work to apply morphometric analysis to detect injuries especially for the vertebrae with conditions like osteoporosis, fractures and implants. Our work is currently focused on improving the segmentation accuracy by experimenting with better and automatic initialization using vertebrae corners [18,19] and/or endplates [5].

References

1. Platzer, P., Hauswirth, N., Jaindl, M., Chatwani, S., Vecsei, V., Gaebler, C.: Delayed or missed diagnosis of cervical spine injuries. J. Trauma Acute Care Surg. **61**(1), 150–155 (2006)
2. Davis, J.W., Phreaner, D.L., Hoyt, D.B., Mackersie, R.C.: The etiology of missed cervical spine injuries. J. Trauma Acute Care Surg. **34**(3), 342–346 (1993)
3. Benjelloun, M., Mahmoudi, S., Lecron, F.: A framework of vertebra segmentation using the active shape model-based approach. J. Biomed. Imaging **2011**, 9 (2011)
4. Mahmoudi, S.A., Lecron, F., Manneback, P., Benjelloun, M., Mahmoudi, S.: GPU-based segmentation of cervical vertebra in X-ray images. In: 2010 IEEE International Conference on Cluster Computing Workshops and Posters (CLUSTER WORKSHOPS), pp. 1–8. IEEE (2010)
5. Roberts, M.G., Cootes, T.F., Adams, J.E.: Automatic location of vertebrae on DXA images using random forest regression. In: Ayache, N., Delingette, H., Golland, P., Mori, K. (eds.) MICCAI 2012. LNCS, vol. 7512, pp. 361–368. Springer, Heidelberg (2012). doi:10.1007/978-3-642-33454-2_45
6. Roberts, M.G., Cootes, T.F., Adams, J.E.: Vertebral shape: automatic measurement with dynamically sequenced active appearance models. In: Duncan, J.S., Gerig, G. (eds.) MICCAI 2005. LNCS, vol. 3750, pp. 733–740. Springer, Heidelberg (2005). doi:10.1007/11566489_90
7. Roberts, M.G., Cootes, T.F., Pacheco, E., Oh, T., Adams, J.E.: Segmentation of lumbar vertebrae using part-based graphs and active appearance models. In: Yang, G.-Z., Hawkes, D., Rueckert, D., Noble, A., Taylor, C. (eds.) MICCAI 2009. LNCS, vol. 5762, pp. 1017–1024. Springer, Heidelberg (2009). doi:10.1007/978-3-642-04271-3_123
8. Roberts, M., Pacheco, E., Mohankumar, R., Cootes, T., Adams, J.: Detection of vertebral fractures in DXA VFA images using statistical models of appearance and a semi-automatic segmentation. Osteoporos. Int. **21**(12), 2037–2046 (2010)
9. Casciaro, S., Massoptier, L.: Automatic vertebral morphometry assessment. In: 29th Annual International Conference of the IEEE on Engineering in Medicine and Biology Society, EMBS 2007, pp. 5571–5574. IEEE (2007)
10. Larhmam, M.A., Mahmoudi, S., Benjelloun, M.: Semi-automatic detection of cervical vertebrae in X-ray images using generalized hough transform. In: 2012 3rd International Conference on Image Processing Theory, Tools and Applications (IPTA), pp. 396–401. IEEE (2012)
11. Larhmam, M.A., Benjelloun, M., Mahmoudi, S.: Vertebra identification using template matching modelmp and K-means clustering. Int. J. Comput. Assist. Radiol. Surg. **9**(2), 177–187 (2014)
12. Cootes, T.F., Taylor, C.J., Cooper, D.H., Graham, J.: Active shape models-their training and application. Comput. Vis. Image Underst. **61**(1), 38–59 (1995)
13. Cootes, T., Taylor, C.: Statistical models of appearance for computer vision, wolfson image anal. unit, univ. manchester, manchester. Technical report, UK (1999)
14. Van Ginneken, B., Frangi, A.F., Staal, J.J., Romeny, B.M., Viergever, M.A.: Active shape model segmentation with optimal features. IEEE Trans. Med. Imaging **21**(8), 924–933 (2002)
15. Cristinacce, D., Cootes, T.F.: Boosted regression active shape models. In: BMVC, vol. 1, p. 7 (2007)

16. Zheng, Y., Barbu, A., Georgescu, B., Scheuering, M., Comaniciu, D.: Four-chamber heart modeling and automatic segmentation for 3-D cardiac CT volumes using marginal space learning and steerable features. IEEE Trans. Med. Imag. **27**(11), 1668–1681 (2008)
17. Bromiley, P., Adams, J., Cootes, T.: Localisation of vertebrae on DXA images using constrained local models with random forest regression voting. In: Yao, J., Glocker, B., Klinder, T., Li, S. (eds.) Recent Advances in Computational Methods and Clinical Applications for Spine Imaging, pp. 159–171. Springer, Switzerland (2015)
18. Masudur Rahman Al-Arif, S.M., Asad, M., Knapp, K., Gundry, M., Slabaugh, G.: Hough forest-based corner detection for cervical spine radiographs. In: Proceedings of the 19th Conference on Medical Image Understanding and Analysis (MIUA), pp. 183–188 (2015)
19. Masudur Rahman Al-Arif, S.M., Asad, M., Knapp, K., Gundry, M., Slabaugh, G.: Cervical vertebral corner detection using Haar-like features and modified Hough forest. In: 2015 5th International Conference on Image Processing Theory, Tools and Applications (IPTA). IEEE (2015)
20. Breiman, L.: Random forests. Mach. Learn. **45**(1), 5–32 (2001)
21. Gall, J., Yao, A., Razavi, N., Van Gool, L., Lempitsky, V.: Hough forests for object detection, tracking, and action recognition. IEEE Trans. Pattern Anal. Mach. Intell. **33**(11), 2188–2202 (2011)

Machine Learning Based Bone Segmentation in Ultrasound

Nora Baka[1]([⊠]), Sieger Leenstra[2], and Theo van Walsum[1]([⊠])

[1] Biomedical Imaging Group Rotterdam,
Department of Radiology & Nuclear Medicine and Medical Informatics,
Erasmus MC, University Medical Center Rotterdam, Rotterdam, The Netherlands
{n.baka,t.vanwalsum}@erasmusmc.nl
[2] Department of Neurosurgery,
Erasmus MC, University Medical Center Rotterdam, Rotterdam, The Netherlands

Abstract. Ultrasound (US) guidance is of increasing interest for minimally invasive procedures in orthopedics due to its safety and cost benefits. However, bone segmentation from US images remains a challenge due to the low signal to noise ratio and artifacts that hamper US images. We propose to learn the appearance of bone-soft tissue interfaces from annotated training data, and present results with two classifiers, structured forest and a cascaded logistic classifier. We evaluated the proposed methods on 143 spinal images from two datasets acquired at different sites. We achieved a segmentation recall of 0.9 and precision 0.91 for the better dataset, and a recall and precision of 0.87 and 0.81 for the combined dataset, demonstrating the potential of the framework.

1 Introduction

Ultrasound (US) guidance is of increasing interest for minimally invasive procedures in orthopedics due to its safety and cost benefits compared to the more conventional X-ray guidance systems. However, bony structure segmentation from US images remains a challenge due to the low signal to noise ratio and artifacts that hamper US images. In this work we propose to learn the appearance of the bone-soft tissue interface from annotated training data, we propose novel features for robust classification, and show its performance on 143 images from two datasets.

In the literature several heuristic techniques have been published for US bone segmentation. In these works a cost function was manually constructed based on the image appearance. Kowal et al. utilized the fact that bones, after an intensity correction that took the expected depth of the bone into account, have the brightest intensity on the image [8]. This approach works well if the depth of the bone is known and no other tissue interfaces are close by, it is though prone to fail in a less controlled imaging setup. Hacihaliloglu et al. proposed to use phase symmetry of the image in the frequency domain [4]. This approach highlights lines and step edges irrespective of image intensity and is therefore well suited for bones at variable depths. It is though not possible to distinguish bone interfaces

© Springer International Publishing AG 2016
J. Yao et al. (Eds.): CSI 2016, LNCS 10182, pp. 16–25, 2016.
DOI: 10.1007/978-3-319-55050-3_2

from other bright interfaces. The feature most widely used to detect bone interface is shadowing, which is caused by the reflection of nearly the entire sound wave by the bone. Karamalis et al. [7] proposed a shadow term which was then incorporated in the above framework by Quader et al. [9], showing improved results. Jain et al. proposed a Bayesian framework for bone segmentation, with the following features: intensity, gradient, shadow, intensity profile along scanline, and multiple reflections [5]. Obtaining the correct conditional probabilities used in the framework is though not straightforward. Foroughi et al. heuristically combined intensity, shadow, and the Laplacian filtered image for creating a bone probability map, which was then segmented with a dynamic programming framework [3]. Jia et al. [6] extended this work by including further feature images such as integrated backscatter, local energy, phase and feature symmetry. All features were normalized and multiplied to derive the bone probability image. As opposed to the heuristic bone probability calculations in literature, we propose to learn the bone probability map from a set of training examples.

Machine learning has been widely used for medical image segmentation, such as in brain MRI, prostate US, etc. Conventionally, such approaches segment a structure with a specific intensity and texture profile, surrounded by a closed contour. Bone interface segmentation in US is different, as here only the outer reflection is visible. Nevertheless, this bone interface has specific features which make it a good candidate for machine learning algorithms. We propose a set of features in this paper and show the accuracy we can achieve with them.

The purpose of this study thus was to answer the following questions. (1) Is it possible to learn a discriminative classifier for bone interfaces in US? (2) Are the features used in the literature robust to different scanning protocols? (3) What accuracy can we achieve with such a system? We address these questions using two 2D spine datasets acquired at different hospitals with different protocols.

2   Methods

The full segmentation framework is shown in Fig. 1. After pre-processing we computed features to discriminate bone from soft tissue interfaces. We used both standard and novel features as described in Sect. 2.2. These features were fed into a classifier to produce a bone probability map. We investigated two types of classifiers, namely pixel-wise and region based classifiers. As a post-processing step dynamic programming was used to produce the final segmentation.

2.1   Pre-processing

We applied two pre-processing steps. First, a Gaussian blurring produces the blurred image I_σ. We empirically found that a standard deviation of $\sigma = 0.3\,\mathrm{mm}$ worked well, smoothing the speckle pattern but still allowing to distinguish adjacent tissue interfaces. A typical speckle size in the depth direction of our images was about 0.1 mm. Second, oblique edges appear with less contrast in the images as only part of the reflected sound reaches the transducer. We propose to enhance

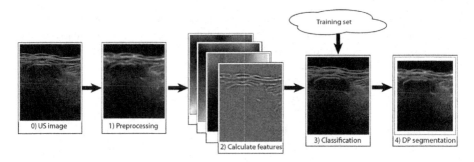

Fig. 1. The schematic method for classification based bone segmentation.

oblique regions with template matching. We took as template the Gabor filter with orientations of 45° and −45°, wavelength $\lambda = 2$ mm, and Gaussian width $\sigma_g = 1$ mm. These parameters were set such that the filter resembles a single oblique edge with some room for deviation from the above angles. The filtered images were then thresholded for retaining only the high score regions, and added to the blurred image such that

$$I_{pre} = I_\sigma + \delta\, F\left(Gabor(\lambda, \sigma_g, 45°) * I_\sigma\right) + \delta\, F(Gabor(\lambda, \sigma_g, -45°) * I_\sigma), \quad (1)$$

where I_{pre} is the final pre-processed image, and F is representing a thresholding with 2, and a subsequent Gaussian blurring with σ. The threshold value was selected empirically, such that only the strongest responses remained, and the subsequent blurring was used to smooth the edges. We used an $\delta = 10$ weighting, such that the maximum value of the enhancement was about 50 for an image with maximum intensity of 255. Examples of original and pre-processed images are shown in Figs. 1 and 2.

2.2   Features

We used standard bone features from the literature, namely

1. Intensity of the pre-processed image I_{pre}.
2. Laplacian of Gaussian (LoG) image $I_{LoG} = -(LoG * I_{pre})$, with scale σ.
3. Intensity shadow, which was calculated as the cumulative sum of image intensities from bottom to top, scaled with the pixel size of the image.
4. Depth. This feature is the distance in mm-s from the transducer, and is mainly used to discard the structures too close to the transducer.

In addition to these standard features, we defined the following novel features.

5. Border-to-border distance. This feature discriminates bright lines based on their length. Lines that run from the left edge of the field of view (FOV) all the way to the right edge will have a lower value than shorter lines and areas without line-like structures. We use the Laplacian of Gaussian image

for enhancing bright line structures. Subsequently, we calculate the weighted distance function from the left border and the right border of the image respectively, where the weight image is $I_{weight} = 1/(\max(0, I_{LoG}) + 0.01)$. The sum of the left and right distances results in low values for pixels that participate in a long structure, and higher values for short lines. It is useful if we know that the imaged bone width is less then the FOV, which is the case with most bones.

6. Centrality. This feature urges the classifier to find structures that are closer to the center column of the field of view, as those structures tend to be of greater importance than the ones on the border. We calculate this feature as the weighted distance function from the center column of the image in both directions. The same weight image I_{weight} was used as in the border-to-border distance.

All feature images except depth were normalized by division by their maximum value. Depth was normalized by division by 30, so that depth values were between 0–2. In addition, the shadow feature images were translated 1 mm to the top, in order to sample the cumulative shadow without the possibly bright bone interface. An example showing all feature images can be seen in Fig. 2.

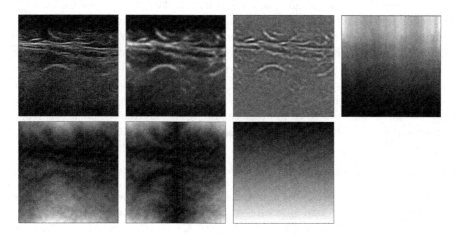

Fig. 2. Feature images from left to right: Original image, pre-processed image, LoG image, intensity shadow, border-to-border distance, centrality and depth.

2.3 Classifiers

We compared two classifiers in this work. For the pixel-wise classification we chose the logistic classifier, as more flexible classifiers quickly overfit. For region based classification we chose structured forests, as it showed promising results on edge detection in natural images [2]. The following paragraphs describe both classifiers in detail.

Logistic Classifier. To make better use of the training data, we implemented a cascade classifier scheme. In the first step, we discarded all regions that did not contain structure, by a hysteresis threshold $HysThr(I_{LoG}, 0.2, 0.03)$ of the normalized I_{LoG} feature. In the second step, a logistic classifier was trained on the pixels remaining after the first step. Negative samples were collected from locations passing the first cascade step, and being further than 2 mm from the ground truth. We sampled all positive samples (typically 200–400 samples), and 5000 negative samples from each training image. We then used weighting to balance the influence of both classes on the decision boundary.

Structured Forest. The structured forest (SF) classifier introduced for edge detection in natural images by [2] was used in this work. It is a random forest classifier where the input and output are patches rather than pixels. We replaced the original RGBD input channels with the feature images described in Sect. 2.2. The feature pool is calculated from these channels by sampling pixels from the patch, and by calculating the difference of any two pixels in the patch after down-sampling it to a size of 5×5. The 6 channels with a patch size of 32 pixels thereby produce 3336 feature candidates for the forest. The intermediate mapping used for the splitting criterion of the tree nodes works best if areas under, and above the bone interface have different labels. We therefore dilated the ground truth downwards with 5 pixels to form the foreground segmentation. Training patches were only sampled from locations where $I_{LoG} > 0.3$ to avoid sampling locations with no structure. We trained a forest of 4 trees and three scale levels, using $1e5$ positive and $2e5$ negative samples. All further parameters were set as proposed in [2]. The output image that results after applying the tree to an unseen US image was blurred according to the scale, and added up to result the forest output. To counteract the intensity loss due to spacial blurring, we then normalized the image to have the highest probability equal to 100.

2.4 Dynamic Programming Segmentation

The classification step produces a probability map of the expected bone interface in the image. To get a final smooth segmentation, we use this probability map and dynamic programming similar to [3], with the cost function $C = C_{intern} + C_{extern}$. The internal energy is created as

$$C_{intern} = 1 - P_{bone}, \tag{2}$$

with an extra line added to the cost image with value 0.6. The segmentation is at this line if there is no bony structure in the image column. The external energy consists of the penalty for moving between columns, as follows:

$$C_{extern} = \begin{cases} jumpCost, & \text{if jump from or to extra line} \\ \alpha(i_{rowCurr} - i_{rowNext})^2, & \text{with maximum 3 rows difference} \end{cases} \tag{3}$$

We used $jumpCost = 1$ and $\alpha = 0.1$ in our experiments.

3   Data

We used two sets of 2D ultrasound images in this study.

Dataset 1 consisted of a training set of 106 vertebra images of 15 subjects (Dataset 1A) and a test set of 56 images of 10 subjects (Dataset1B), acquired at the Tilburg Hospital with a 2D Philips L12-3 Broadband linear array transducer. Every vertebra was imaged for about 3 sec at a gain of 45, contrast 55, and base imaging depth of 5 cm. This depth was adjusted if needed. The patient was imaged in a supine position. For every vertebra one image of the sequence was selected for manual annotation of the ground truth bone surfaces.

Dataset 2 consisted of a training set of 91 vertebra images of 11 subjects (Dataset 2A) and a test set of 87 images of 10 subjects (Dataset 2B), acquired at Erasmus MC, with a Philips iU22 machine and the 2D L12-5 linear transducer. The images were acquired with the general musculo-skeletal protocol, with imaging depth adjusted between 3–5 cm depending on the patient, and gain 65. Focus was adjusted so that the imaged bone should be in the focus region. Pixel size in most cases was around 0.1 mm. SonoCT and XRES adaptive image enhancement were switched on. The patient was imaged in a sitting position. The patient population consisted of back-pain patients of ages between 19 and 77, with BMI between 17.9 and 39.1. For every vertebra one image of the sequence was selected for manual annotation of the ground truth bone surfaces.

Manual annotation was done by spline interpolation between manually placed control-points in both datasets. In every image only one vertebra was annotated. In dataset 1 due to the smaller field of view of the transducer this meant all visible bony structures were segmented. In dataset 2 with a larger field of view in about half of the cases the edge of neighboring vertebral processes were also visible, these were not included in the ground truth segmentation.

4   Experiments and Results

We performed experiments to (a) evaluate the accuracy of the two classifiers and their segmentation performance; (b) assess the robustness of the methods to different acquisition setups; (c) compare the method with the method of Foroughi [3]. Comparison with Foroughi was only performed on dataset 1, as there all bony structures were segmented in the ground truth. To evaluate the performance of the classifiers and the subsequent dynamic programming segmentation, we used recall, precision, and the F-measure as follows:

- Classifier recall (Rec_C): The ratio of ground truth contour that was classified correctly and the length of the entire contour.
- Classifier precision ($Prec_C$): The ratio of detection inside the dilated ground truth compared to all detections.
- Segmentation recall (Rec_S): the number segmentation points inside the dilated ground truth region, divided by the number of ground truth pixels. As every column has maximum one pixel marked as bone interface, this results in a normalized number, such that the perfect contour has sensitivity 1, and if

bone was not found, sensitivity is 0. However, sensitivity might also be larger than 1 due to the region enlargement. Values larger than 1 are thresholded to 1.

- Segmentation precision ($Prec_S$). The length of the segmentation inside the dilated ground truth divided by the total length of the segmentation.
- F-measure: The F-measure is the harmonic mean of precision and recall: $F = 2\frac{prec \cdot rec}{prec + rec}$. The combination of these two measures facilitates the comparison of classifier accuracies.

Dilation for the ground truth was set to 2 mm where dilation was used.

The threshold value used to calculate the classification evaluation measures was set to 50% for the logistic classifier, and to 30% for the structured forest classifier. These values were optimized based on the training set. For the dynamic programming the parameter values are mentioned in Sect. 2.4. These parameters were optimized on the Foroughi method with training set A, and were used for all experiments in this paper.

The results of the experiments are shown in Table 1. Besides the average precision and recall we also report the number of failures, defined by a segmentation precision or recall < 0.01. Figure 3 shows examples of bone probability images and their segmentation using the relative shadow feature.

Table 1. Classification and segmentation results of the proposed framework on the test set, together with results of the method of Foroughi et al. [3]. 1 and 2 denote the two different ultrasound datasets used in this paper, 1A2A and 1B2B denotes the combined training and test dataset respectively.

Classifier	Train	Test	Segmentation			Classification			
			Recall	Precision	F-meas	F-meas	Recall	Precision	#fail
Logistic	1A	1B	0.93	0.76	0.84	0.77	0.87	0.69	1
Logistic	2A	2B	0.93	0.59	0.72	0.70	0.87	0.59	1
Logistic	1A	2B	0.85	0.39	0.53	0.45	0.89	0.30	6
Logistic	2A	1B	0.62	0.61	0.62	0.63	0.56	0.71	12
Logistic	1A2A	1B2B	0.89	0.57	0.69	0.64	0.87	0.50	7
SF	1A	1B	0.90	0.91	0.90	0.85	0.84	0.87	0
SF	2A	2B	0.83	0.80	0.80	0.78	0.77	0.79	6
SF	1A	2B	0.78	0.61	0.66	0.65	0.76	0.57	10
SF	2A	1B	0.58	0.69	0.61	0.62	0.58	0.67	8
SF	1A2A	1B2B	0.87	0.81	0.82	0.80	0.82	0.79	4
Foroughi		1B	0.71	0.67	0.66				6

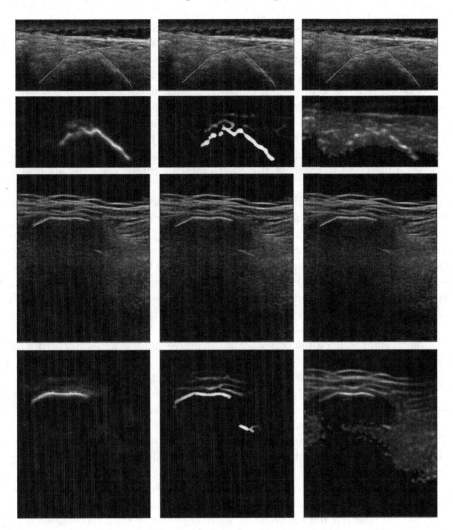

Fig. 3. Example images and segmentations from dataset 1. From left to right: Structured forest, Logistic classifier, and Foroughi et al. [3]. The original images with ground truth (blue) and dynamic programming segmentations (red) are in the odd rows. The corresponding probability images are in the even rows. (Color figure online)

5   Discussion and Conclusions

We performed experiments evaluating bone interface classification and segmentation from US images in two datasets (Table 1). The two datasets were acquired on different machines and with different protocols. Though visually the images looked similar in the two datasets, the low cross-evaluation accuracy (F measure between 0.45 and 0.65) shows that the statistical properties of the two datasets were different. The largest difference we found in the histogram of the shadow feature, which showed a clear difference in the optimal threshold value for separation of bone and non-bone interfaces in the two datasets.

We also found that structured forest with the relative probability threshold consistently achieved higher accuracy than the logistic classifier (with a difference between 8–20 % F-measure). Notably, the SF classifier on the combined dataset achieved an accuracy close to the average accuracy of the purely trained classifiers. This might be due to the selection of the best features during training, the non-linear decision boundary, and the use of regional information. This result is important, as it suggests, that a smart classifier may compensate for statistical differences in datasets, thereby facilitating robust generally applicable methods.

We also looked at the failure cases in the combined dataset experiment. The structured forest classifier failed on four cases. All four cases were from dataset 2. Two failures were images of short bones far from the FOV center. These were not detected. One image contained two vertebrae. As only one of them was annotated in the ground truth, and the other one was segmented by the method, it counted as a complete failure. The last failure was due to a wrong FOV cropping. There were 80 zero-padded columns on the right of the image, which interfered with the way the border-to-border feature is calculated. In lack of this feature the fat-muscle interfaces were segmented instead of the bone-soft-tissue interface. Generally, bright well visible bones with distinctive shadow are segmented with the highest confidence.

Comparing segmentation and classification performances, segmentation may outperform classification. This is possibly due to the added smoothness and spatial connectedness constraints that help to ignore small false positive and negative classifications. All dynamic programming segmentation experiments were performed with the same parameters, optimized for the method of Foroughi [3]. Further improvements might be possible with specially tuned parameter values for the different datasets.

We also compared our results with the method of Foroughi et al. [3]. Both the logistic and structured forest classifiers outperformed this heuristic approach. We also conclude that our dataset must be more challenging than the dataset used in the original paper, as the results are substantially worse than the reported ones.

The computation time of the structured forest, with an implementation based on the optimized Matlab code of [1,2], took 0.5 s, and the subsequent dynamic programming another 0.2 s. The logistic classifier was implemented in Python 2.7 using scikit-learn package without speed related optimization. The classifier including the dynamic programming thereby took 2.6 s to compute on a laptop with intel i7-2760QM 2.4 GHz cpu and 16 GB ram.

We conclude that machine learning is a feasible and accurate way for bone segmentation in ultrasound. We achieved best results with the structured forest segmentation scheme with recall and precision as high as 0.90/0.91 on dataset A, and 0.87/0.81 on the combined dataset.

Acknowledgement. The authors were financially supported by the Dutch Science Foundation STW, project number 14542. The authors would furthermore like to thank Marcel Toorop and Eelke Bos for their help in data annotation.

References

1. Dollár, P.: Piotr's Computer Vision Matlab Toolbox (PMT) (2016)
2. Dollár, P., Zitnick, C.L.: Structured forests for fast edge detection. In: 2013 IEEE International Conference on Computer Vision, pp. 1841–1848. IEEE, December 2013
3. Foroughi, P., Boctor, E., Swartz, M.J., Taylor, R.H., Fichtinger, G.: Ultrasound bone segmentation using dynamic programming. In: 2007 IEEE Ultrasonics Symposium Proceedings, pp. 2523–2526. IEEE, October 2007
4. Hacihaliloglu, I., Abugharbieh, R., Hodgson, A., Rohling, R.: Bone segmentation and fracture detection in ultrasound using 3D local phase features. In: Metaxas, D., Axel, L., Fichtinger, G., Székely, G. (eds.) MICCAI 2008. LNCS, vol. 5241, pp. 287–295. Springer, Heidelberg (2008). doi:10.1007/978-3-540-85988-8_35
5. Jain, A.K., Taylor, R.H.: Understanding bone responses in B-mode ultrasound images and automatic bone surface extraction using a Bayesian probabilistic framework. In: Walker, W.F., Emelianov, S.Y. (eds.) SPIE Medical Imaging, pp. 131–142. International Society for Optics and Photonics, April 2004
6. Jia, R., Mellon, S.J., Hansjee, S., Monk, A.P., Murray, D.W., Noble, J.A.: Automatic bone segmentation in ultrasound images using local phase features and dynamic programming. In: 2016 IEEE 13th International Symposium on Biomedical Imaging (ISBI), pp. 1005–1008. IEEE, April 2016
7. Karamalis, A., Wein, W., Klein, T., Navab, N.: Ultrasound confidence maps using random walks. Med. Image Anal. **16**(6), 1101–1112 (2012)
8. Kowal, J., Amstutz, C., Langlotz, F., Talib, H., Ballester, M.G.: Automated bone contour detection in ultrasound B-mode images for minimally invasive registration in computer-assisted surgery—anin vitro evaluation. Int. J. Med. Robot. Comput. Assist. Surg. **3**(4), 341–348 (2007)
9. Quader, N., Hodgson, A., Abugharbieh, R.: Confidence weighted local phase features for robust bone surface segmentation in ultrasound. In: Linguraru, M.G., et al. (eds.) CLIP 2014. LNCS, vol. 8680, pp. 76–83. Springer, Cham (2014). doi:10.1007/978-3-319-13909-8_10

Variational Segmentation of the White and Gray Matter in the Spinal Cord Using a Shape Prior

Antal Horváth[1]([✉]), Simon Pezold[1], Matthias Weigel[1,2], Katrin Parmar[3], Oliver Bieri[1,2], and Philippe Cattin[1]

[1] Department of Biomedical Engineering, University of Basel, Allschwil, Switzerland
antal.horvath@unibas.ch
[2] Radiological Physics, Clinics of Radiology,
University Hospital Basel, Basel, Switzerland
[3] Department of Neurology, University Hospital Basel, Basel, Switzerland

Abstract. Segmenting the inner structure of the spinal cord on magnetic resonance (MR) images is difficult because of poor contrast between white and gray matter (WM/GM). We present a variational formulation to automatically detect cerebrospinal fluid and WM/GM. The segmentation results are obtained by continuous cuts combined with a shape prior. Intensity-based segmentation guarantees high accuracy while the shape prior aims at precision. We tested the algorithm on a set of MR images with visual WM/GM contrast and evaluated it w.r.t. manual GM segmentations. The automated GM segmentations are on a par with the manual results.

1 Introduction

Numerous neurological diseases manifest not only in the brain but also in the spinal cord (SC). Accurate SC segmentation recently gained increasing attention. Measuring the SC cross-sectional area on magnetic resonance (MR) images has shown to be a good quantitative measure to study diseases of the central nervous system like multiple sclerosis (MS). MS shows strong influence on the SC, which manifests e.g. in atrophy and lesion formation [7]. Spinal cord atrophy is occurring early in the disease progress and was shown to correlate very well with the clinical evaluation (EDSS) of the patient i.e. with MS disability progression [7]. Especially the SC gray matter area was shown to correlate strongly with MS disability [11].

Delineating white (WM) and gray matter (GM) and measuring their areas or volumes in-vivo is challenging because of their fine structure, poor WM/GM imaging contrast, limited practical MR resolution, and inter- and intrapatient variability of the captured images and of the SCs themselves. On top of that, high intra- and interobserver variability in manual segmentations make further statistical evaluations difficult.

To overcome these challenges and to further deepen the knowledge about the GM/WM atrophy in the SC an automatic quantitative segmentation method is required that has high accuracy as well as precision.

© Springer International Publishing AG 2016
J. Yao et al. (Eds.): CSI 2016, LNCS 10182, pp. 26–37, 2016.
DOI: 10.1007/978-3-319-55050-3_3

Given an MR image with optimal contrast and signal-to-noise ratio, an intensity-based segmentation method is perfectly suited for that job. The more noise is involved the more we need to regularize the method. To handle partial volume effects of captured fine structures, even shape priors may be necessary.

Yiannakas et al. [16] show the feasibility of segmenting WM/GM in the SC. Tang et al. [12] use a Bayesian three-class classifier, and Asman et al. [1] use groupwise multi-atlas segmentation to discriminate WM/GM slice-wise. Taso et al. [13] construct atlases for cerebrospinal fluid (CSF), WM/GM and propose atlas based 3D segmentation and classification methods. De Leener et al. [5] provide a more comprehensive review of the available GM segmentation methods. However, no standard method has yet been established, which motivates the search for alternative approaches.

In this paper, we propose an automatic variational segmentation method that can locate CSF and segment the WM/GM of the spinal cord. We describe our data in Sect. 2, introduce our generic models in Sect. 3, show the results in Sect. 4, and discuss them in Sect. 5.

2   Data

For this paper 10 volunteers (6 male, 4 female) were scanned with an experimental MR sequence (approved by the local ethics review board). In total we acquired 16 axial cross-sectional sets of images on C3 level with acceptable WM/GM contrast using a 2D-MOLLI sequence [15] with $0.4 \times 0.4\,\text{mm}^2$ in-plane resolution and 8 mm slice thickness. The MOLLI sequence acquires altogether 11 aligned images in each image set with different inversion times TI per slice [15]. The first image of each image set has good CSF contrast and the average of each set has good WM/GM contrast. In Fig. 1 we see the first three images and the mean image of one set. Figure 3 shows more mean images of different contrast quality and of different subjects.

Two experienced raters segmented the 16 images manually for GM. Rater 1 rated two times at different days with different techniques. In one technique images in the original resolution were segmented pixel-wise, see Fig. 3. In the other, 10-fold upsampled cubic interpolated images were segmented whose masks were downsampled again afterwards. The second technique resulted in a grayscale segmentation. Rater 2 used the same up- and downsampling technique.

3   Method

In this paper we present a variational approach that segments CSF, WM, GM, and background given a set of MR images of the same slice. Because binary segmentation algorithms are more robust than multi-labeling algorithms and because of the special situation of the MOLLI sequence, where the first image has good CSF contrast, we split our fully automatic approach into two steps: a CSF segmentation step and a WM/GM segmentation step. The second step

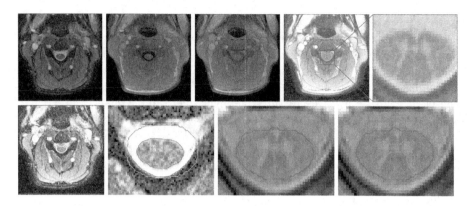

Fig. 1. *Upper row:* first three images of the MOLLI sequence of a cross-sectional neck scan on C3 level; histogram-equalized mean image and its zoom depict CSF, WM, GM. *Lower row, segmentation steps:* CSF contrast image with ellipsoidal prior; zoomed view on the CSF segmentation (*red*) and mask (*yellow*); GM segmentation (*green*) and the boundary towards CSF (*red*) before and after shape regularization. (Color figure online)

makes use of the previously labeled CSF, where we extract the interior of the ring-shaped CSF and use it as a mask for the WM/GM discrimination, see Fig. 1.

In recent years a tendency towards relaxed convex variational formulations can be observed because their solutions all enjoy to have the optimal score. The motivation of using continuous cuts [17] lies in the mathematical beauty and in the simple algorithmic implementation. The model is convex and finds intended segmentations robustly, independent of any specific algorithm initialization. Its dual formulation, also called continuous max flow, has analogies to graph cut [3], but enables subpixel accuracy and has less metrication errors. We added different additional features to the continuous cut formulation: anisotropic total variation (ATV) [8], pose invariant shape priors [4,9], an additive Bhattacharyya coefficient (BC) [14], and prior boundary curvature dependent capacities.

3.1   Mathematical Ingredients

Before we describe the CSF and WM/GM segmentation steps, we first introduce continuous cuts [17] and additional energies, which we use in both steps.

The most basic segmentation method is intensity thresholding, where the pixels are divided into two categories: those with intensity values lower and respectively higher than a certain threshold. Because of the presence of noise in high resolution MR images, before thresholding, first an approximation of the image has to be calculated where the noise is reduced. In the literature this problem can be modeled with the Mumford-Shah functional [2]. We make use of a generalized special case of the piecewise-constant Mumford-Shah problem

$$\underset{\mathcal{O} \subset \Omega}{\mathrm{argmin}} \int_{\mathcal{O}} C_t(x)\, dx + \int_{\Omega \setminus \mathcal{O}} C_s(x)\, dx + \mathrm{TV}_C(\partial \mathcal{O}), \tag{1}$$

which is also a generalized version of the Chan-Vese model and can be seen as a generic segmentation model [17]: Inside the image domain Ω the object $\mathcal{O}$ and the background $\mathcal{B} := \Omega \backslash \mathcal{O}$ shall be found, where C_t, C_s and C are the model parameters, here called capacity functions. The name *capacity* and the indices of C_s and C_t find their roots in graph cuts and stand for source and target. C_t has to be low on the object $\mathcal{O}$, and C_s has to be low in the background.

For an associated algorithm to be automatic, it is necessary to estimate proper capacity functions automatically. In this task, mean intensity differences turned out to be well-suited for the terminal capacities C_s and C_t. For non-terminal capacities C we chose negative exponential image gradients. The weighted total variation TV_C as an object boundary length regularizer can be adapted anisotropically to the image structures when introducing a Riemannian metric tensor A [8], replacing TV_C by ATV_C.

To find a convex version of the above functional (1) one introduces a relaxed labeling $u : \Omega \to [0,1]$, such that x is in $\mathcal{O}$ if $u(x)$ is close to 1 and x is in $\mathcal{B}$ if $u(x)$ is close to 0. This way we can write down the continuous cut with ATV

$$\operatorname*{argmin}_{u:\Omega \to [0,1]} \int_\Omega C_t(x)u(x) + C_s(x)(1-u(x)) + C(x)\,\|\nabla u(x)\|_A \; dx, \qquad (2)$$

where $\|\nabla u(x)\|_A = \sqrt{\nabla u(x)^T A(x) \nabla u(x)} = \left\| S(x)^T \nabla u(x) \right\|_2$, and $A = SS^T$ is a strongly positive definite, matrix valued function [8]. Olsson et al. [8] proofed that a coarea formula for ATV holds and thus a thresholding theorem exists for solutions of (2). This means that for a minimizer $u^\star$ of (2) and any threshold θ in $]0,1]$ the thresholded superlevel set $\mathbb{1}_{u^\star \geq \theta}$ is again a minimizer of (2).

Algorithms that minimize (2) itself may struggle with the non-differentiability of $\|\nabla u(x)\|_2$ twofold: the non-differentiability of $\|\cdot\|_2$ at the origin and the calculation of ∇u along jump-parts. A nice work-around is provided by the primal-dual formulation of (2). As proposed in [10], adding an augmented Lagrangian and calculating the variational derivatives results in a very short algorithm: We iterate a valid initialization (p_s^0, p_t^0, p^0, u^0) with

$$\begin{aligned}
p_s^{k+1} &= \min\left((1-u^k)/c + \operatorname{div} Sp^k + p_t^k,\, C_s\right), \\
p_t^{k+1} &= \min\left(u^k/c - \operatorname{div} Sp^k + p_s^{k+1},\, C_t\right), \\
p^{k+1} &= \mathcal{P}\left(p^k + \gamma\, S^T\, \nabla\left(\operatorname{div} Sp^k - p_s^{k+1} + p_t^{k+1} - u^k/c\right)\right), \\
u^{k+1} &= u^k - c\left(\operatorname{div} Sp^{k+1} - p_s^{k+1} + p_t^{k+1}\right),
\end{aligned} \qquad (3)$$

where $\mathcal{P}(p(x)) = \operatorname{sign}(p(x)) \min(|p(x)|, C(x))$. We use $c = 0.3$ and $\gamma = 0.16$.

Up to here the model is convex and fulfills a thresholding theorem. Now we vary the capacity functions and make them dependent on u, thus in general we lose the mathematical global optimality property. In practice, as long as the capacity functions do not change too fast, they converge with u. We lose convexity anyway, as we include additional energy terms like BC [14], and a mean squared difference to a shape prior [4,9], see next sections. Of course, the mathematical properties of the continuous cut in practice still help to balance out the local properties of the additional energies, as long as they are weighted appropriately. In turn, BC helps out the segmentation process to stick to the local intensity structure while the shape prior term includes prior knowledge.

Pose Invariant Shape Prior. Given a grayscale image $I : \Omega \to [0,1]$, a shape prior $f_0 : \Omega \to [0,1]$, and a relaxed labeling u, we introduce the effective image

$$I_{\text{eff}} = \lambda\, I_{\text{model}} + \mu\, I_{\text{prior}}, \quad I_{\text{model}} = c_0\,(1-u) + c_1\,u, \quad I_{\text{prior}} = b_0\,(1-f) + b_1\,f, \quad (4)$$

with c_1 and c_0 the mean intensities of the background and foreground, $f = f_0 \circ T_p : \Omega \to [0,1]$ a rigidly transformed version of f_0, and b_1 and b_0 the mean model intensities on the rigidly transformed shape prior area and its complement [9]. The idea is to minimize

$$\int_\Omega \lambda\,(I - I_{\text{model}})^2 + \mu\,(I_{\text{model}} - I_{\text{prior}})^2 + C\,\|\nabla u\|_A \; dx, \qquad (5)$$

where we segment and force the segmented result to be close to the prior by minimizing the mean squared distance to the relaxed piecewise constant approximation I_{model}. By factoring out with remainder, we see that minimizing the latter is equivalent to minimizing

$$E(u,c,f,b) = \int_\Omega (I_{\text{eff}} - c_1)^2\,u + (I_{\text{eff}} - c_0)^2\,(1-u) + C\,\|\nabla u\|_A \; dx, \qquad (6)$$

which is in the form of a continuous cut, thus can be optimized by (3). In practice, we replace $(I_{\text{eff}}(x) - c_1)^2$ and $(I_{\text{eff}}(x) - c_0)^2$ with functions $C_t(x)$ and $C_s(x)$ that stay close to the idea of (4): The square function is replaced with the absolute function and c_0 and c_1 are varied slightly, see below.

Following [9], the rigid coordinates $p = (a, b, \theta, \exp\sigma)$ of the prior f can be iterated by a gradient descent through

$$a^{n+1} = a^n - \iota\frac{\langle f - u, -\partial_{x_1} f\rangle}{\|f\|^2}, \quad \theta^{n+1} = \theta^n - \iota\frac{\langle f - u, -\nabla f^T J(x - (a,b)^{n+1})\rangle}{\||x - (a,b)|\,\nabla f\|^2},$$

$$b^{n+1} = b^n - \iota\frac{\langle f - u, -\partial_{x_2} f\rangle}{\|f\|^2}, \quad \sigma^{n+1} = \sigma^n - \iota\frac{\langle f - u, -\nabla f^T (x - (a,b)^{n+1})\rangle}{\||x - (a,b)|\,\nabla f\|^2},$$

$$(7)$$

where $J = \left(\begin{smallmatrix} 0 & 1 \\ -1 & 0 \end{smallmatrix}\right)$, and $\langle\cdot,\cdot\rangle$ and $\|\cdot\|$ denote the L^2 scalar product and norm. The denominators, obtained through the metric on the Lie group of the transformed priors, can be seen as automatic step size controllers. We use the stepsize $\iota = 1$.

Bhattacharyya Coefficient. BC is a measure of how different two densities are. The goal of intensity-based segmentation can be described as finding regions with maximally distinct histograms. Given the two histogram densities f_O and f_B of the object and the background with values in Z, their BC is given by

$$BC(f_O, f_B) = \int_Z \sqrt{f_O(z)\,f_B(z)}\; dz. \qquad (8)$$

Following Wang et al. [14] we calculate the variational derivative $\frac{\delta \cdot}{\delta u}$ of BC:

$$\frac{\delta BC}{\delta u}(x) = \frac{1}{2}\delta(u(x) - \theta) \int_{Z} \sqrt{f_O(z)\,f_B(z)} \left(\frac{1}{A_B} - \frac{1}{A_O}\right) +$$

$$+ \delta(I(x) - z)\left(\frac{\sqrt{f_O(z)f_B(z)}}{f_B(z)}\frac{1}{A_O} - \frac{\sqrt{f_O(z)f_B(z)}}{f_O(z)}\frac{1}{A_B}\right) dz,$$

$$\tag{9}$$

where the histograms and the areas A_O and A_B are represented through thresholded u segmentations, and $\delta(\cdot)$ stands for the Dirac-delta distribution. A more global variant of the BC gradient could be calculated by plugging in u directly, omitting the factor $\delta(u(x) - \theta)$ in (9). But since we only want to influence the continuous cut close to the boundary of the thresholded solution, we chose this version. In the algorithm we set θ to 0.5 and use a standard arctan approximation with $\epsilon = 1$ for the δ function outside the integral. Given a discrete image, we already calculate discrete histogram densities which also discretizes $\int_Z dz$ to $\sum_{z \in Z}$ and $\delta(I(x) - z)$ to the Kronecker delta $\delta_{I(x),z}$.

Wang et al. [14] combined the level set representation of the Chan-Vese energy with BC. We now combine the continuous cut energy for shape priors with BC, weighted with a factor ν:

$$\min \int_{\Omega} C_t(u, f, I)\, u + C_s(u, f, I)\, (1 - u) + C(f, I)\, \|\nabla u\|_A \, dx + \nu\, BC(u). \tag{10}$$

With this external energy, the update rule for u in (3) changes to

$$u^{k+1} = \mathcal{P}_u\left(u^k - c\left(\operatorname{div} Sp^{k+1} - p_s^{k+1} + p_t^{k+1} + \nu\frac{\delta BC}{\delta u}\right)\right). \tag{11}$$

The local behavior of the variational derivative of BC is guided by the convex property of the continuous cut. BC influences twofold: For the terminal capacities, aside mean intensity differences, also object and background histogram densities can be used. This choice, in practice, turned out unsuited for automatic segmentation when the object is not already well initialized. Using BC we can incorporate the histogram densities simultaneously with mean intensity differences. The second benefit is: While continuous cut (6) is computing on the effective image I_{eff}, BC is dealing with the original image intensities. BC makes the choice of the capacities less sensitive and balances the influence of the prior in the segmentation process.

Statistical Appearance Model. We do not only want the shape prior f_0 to be a statistical mean shape, but we also want the shape prior to adapt to the actual segmentation. Cremers et al. [4] use an appearance model for this task, because projection and backprojection are low cost compared to a displacement field model, where non-rigid registration is involved. They also showed that optimizing the model parameter inside the set of meaningful parameters is convex.

Let us model the shape priors by a Gaussian distribution with mean f_0 and covariance C and let $C = V\Lambda^2 V^T$ be its eigendecomposition. Following [4], we use our continuous cut energy (10) for an appearance model realization optimization together with an appearance prior regularizer $\xi \alpha^T \Lambda \alpha$:

$$\min_\alpha \int_\Omega C_t f + C_s(1-f) + C \|\nabla f\|_A \, dx + \nu BC(u) + \xi \alpha^T \Lambda \alpha, \qquad (12)$$

with the backprojection $f = f(\alpha, p) = \min(\max(f_0(p) + V(p)\Lambda\alpha, 0), 1)$, where $f_0(p)$ and $V(p)$ are the rigidly transformed mean GM and eigenshapes at the rigid coordinates p.

In (12) compared to (10) $f(\alpha, p)$ takes the role of u and since they have to be similar, we initialize the model parameter α with the projection of u^{k_0}, where u^{k_0} is an acceptable solution of the model (10). We iterate the model parameter simultaneously with projected u-updates from (11):

$$\alpha^0 = \Lambda^{-1} V(p)^T (u^{k_0} - f_0(p)),$$
$$\alpha^{n+1} = \alpha^n - \Delta t_\alpha \Lambda^{-1} V(p)^T \left(\operatorname{div} Sp^{k+1} - p_s^{k+1} + p_t^{k+1} + \nu \frac{\delta BC}{\delta u} \right) - 2\xi\Lambda\alpha^n. \qquad (13)$$

The idea behind this algorithm is: projecting u in every iteration into the model space and using its approximation f as the prior. But since we can choose the stepsize Δt_α, the prior and the segmented structure are, up to the point where f is initialized, uncoupled from each other.

Anisotropic Total Variation. We use the structure tensor of the image to design the Riemannian metric matrix field $A : \Omega \rightarrow \mathbb{R}^{2\times 2}$ [6]. In $\int_\Omega \|\nabla u\|_A \, dx$ we want the integrand to be small at high image gradients. Thus, for each x in Ω the eigenvalue of $A(x)$ in image gradient direction, which is parallel to ∇u, has to be small. Let $B(x)\hat{A}(x)B(x)^T$ be the eigendecomposition of the symmetric structure tensor at point x with decreasing order of eigenvalues and let $\lambda(x)$ denote the larger eigenvalue. We use the gamma-transformed normalized negative transform of all image gradient magnitudes $(1 - N(\lambda)(x))^2$, to scale the image gradient direction, such that ∇u gets less penalized when the image gradient is stronger. We define $S(x) = B(x) \operatorname{diag}((1 - N(\lambda)(x))^2 + \epsilon, 1)$, where we add $\epsilon > 0$ to guarantee strong positiveness of the matrix field. When λ gets small, $(1 - N(\lambda)(x))^2$ tends quadratically to 1, thus A approaches the isotropic identity matrix in regions with weak edges.

Notations and Definitions. For super- and lowerlevel sets we set $\{u \sim \theta\} = \{x \in \Omega \,|\, u(x) \sim \theta\}$, where $\sim$ stands for a relation $(=, >, <, ...)$. We denote the normalization of a real-valued function $v : \Omega \rightarrow \mathbb{R}$ as the function $N(v) : \Omega \rightarrow [0, 1]$ with $N(v)(x) = (v(x) - \min_s v(s))/(\max_s v(s) - \min_s v(s))$, and the normalized gamma transform $\Gamma(v) : \Omega \times \mathbb{R}_+ \rightarrow [0, 1]$ with $\Gamma(v)(x, \gamma) = (N(v)(x))^\gamma$. We denote the shortest Euclidean distance between x and the boundary of $\{f = 1\}$ by $d(x, f)$. $\mathcal{F}_{\text{median}}$ is a median filter of size 3×3. For all the terms that need to be regularized we add a constant $\epsilon = 10^{-5}$. Tolerances have been chosen, such that the L^1 norm of an update is smaller than 1 pixel for 10 consecutive iterations.

3.2 CSF Segmentation

Given a histogram-equalized MR image $I : \Omega \subset \mathbb{R}^2 \to [0, 1]$ with good CSF contrast we introduce an ellipsoidal shape prior $f_0 : \Omega \to \{0, 1\}$, shown in Fig. 2. We use the segmentation model (10) with $\lambda = \mu = 0.5$, $\nu = 0$, and

A while f_0 is being registered:

$$C_s(x) = \mathcal{F}_{\text{median}}(\Gamma(|I_{\text{eff}}(x) - \text{mean}(I(\{f > 0.5\})|, 3/2)),$$
$$C_t(x) = \mathcal{F}_{\text{median}}(\Gamma(|I_{\text{eff}}(x) - \text{mean}(I(\{f \leqslant 0.5\})|, 2/3)),$$
$$C(x) = 1/10 \log(1 + d(x, f)) + \epsilon,$$

B after f_0 has been registered:

$$C_s(x) = \mathcal{F}_{\text{median}}\left(\frac{\max(\log(f_\mathcal{O} + \epsilon) - \log(f_\mathcal{B} + \epsilon), 0)}{\log(1 + \epsilon) - \log \epsilon}\right),$$
$$C_t(x) = \mathcal{F}_{\text{median}}\left(\frac{\max(\log(f_\mathcal{B} + \epsilon) - \log(f_\mathcal{O} + \epsilon), 0)}{\log(1 + \epsilon) - \log \epsilon}\right),$$
$$C(x) = \gamma_1 \exp\left(-\gamma_2 \|\nabla I_{\text{assist}}(x)\|\right).$$

In **A**, the translational initial point of f is the center of mass of the neck, calculated through Otsu's thresholding, which is then iterated through (7). The terminal capacity functions are gamma-transformed with experimentally chosen exponents $3/2$ and $2/3$ to enhance the contrast between object and background. In **B**, when f has been registered to the CSF position, we calculate a mask and use it as the new image domain – marked yellow in Fig. 2. We use the convex hull of the ellipsoid and dilate it with a box-shaped structuring element of size 4, to make sure that the segmentation does not leak into surrounding bright intensity areas, when we switch to other capacity functions. The non-terminal capacity C is then changed to a negative exponential of gradient magnitudes of an assisting image I_{assist}. The assisting image at a bigger TI relaxation time, where the CSF is black and the spinal tract is brighter, helps in case the captured CSF of the subject is not ring-shaped. CSF can be pressed away though the gravity of the spinal tract when lying on the back, compare Fig. 2.

3.3 WM/GM Segmentation

Given an image $I : \Omega \cap M \subset \mathbb{R}^2 \to [0, 1]$ with good WM/GM contrast, the inner part of the segmented CSF as a mask M and a statistical model for GM, we use (10) and (12) with $\lambda = \mu = 0.5$, $\nu = 5$, $\xi = 0$, $\Delta t_\alpha = 0.2$ (13), and

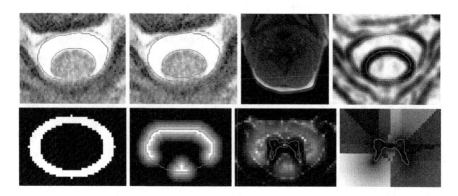

Fig. 2. *Upper row:* CSF segmentation without adapted non-terminal capacity; CSF segmentation with adapted non-terminal capacity; assisting image I_{assist}; adapted non-terminal capacity for CSF – low values along the posterior CSF result in weak length regularization. *Lower row:* Ellipsoidal-shaped CSF prior (major and minor axis roughly 10 mm and 7 mm); special mask M_{special} with high values where GM cannot be; negative exponential of gradient magnitudes combined with M_{special}; negative transformed GM curvature multiplied by distance map. (Color figure online)

A during initial segmentation and rigid registration:

$$C_s(x) = \mathcal{F}_{\text{median}}(\Gamma(|I(x) - \text{mean}(I(M))|, {}^3\!/_2)),$$
$$C_t(x) = \mathcal{F}_{\text{median}}(\Gamma(|I_{\text{eff}}(x) - 0|, {}^2\!/_3)),$$
$$C(x) = g(x) + \frac{\text{median}(g) + \max(g)}{2} \cdot M_{\text{special}}, \quad g(x) = \gamma_1 \exp\left(-\gamma_2 \|\nabla I(x)\|\right),$$

B during appearance model registration:

$$C_s(x) = \mathcal{F}_{\text{median}}(\Gamma(|I_{\text{eff}}(x) - \text{mean}(I(\{f > 0.5\}))|, 4)),$$
$$C_t(x) = \mathcal{F}_{\text{median}}(\Gamma(|I_{\text{eff}}(x) - \text{mean}(I(\{f \leqslant 0.5\}))|, {}^1\!/_4)),$$
$$C(x) = {}^1\!/_{10} \log(1 + d(x, f)) \cdot \zeta(x, f) + \epsilon.$$

The time-domain **A** starts with an initial segmentation according to (10) without a prior. Once the segmentation updates reach the tolerance, the rigid registration part starts. The initial translational coordinate is set to the center of mass of the WM/GM mask M. For C we construct a special mask M_{special}, where capacities are forced to be high in regions where GM cannot be, see Fig. 2.

When the rigid registration and segmentation updates reach the tolerance, time-domain **B** starts. Here the model appearance f is being registered according to (12). We observed that, as long as f is registered appropriately, calculating mean intensities of object and background depending on the prior f seems more stable than looking at the actual areas defined through u. For C_s and C_t, $I_{\text{eff}} = (I_{\text{model}} + I_{\text{prior}})/2$ is replaced with $(I + I_{\text{prior}})/2$, compare (4). This way we combine again unblurred original image intensities with prior information.

With the curvature κ on the boundary of the prior, we define for any point in Ω the normalized negative transform of the curvature $\zeta(x, f) = 1 - N(\kappa)(\hat{x})$

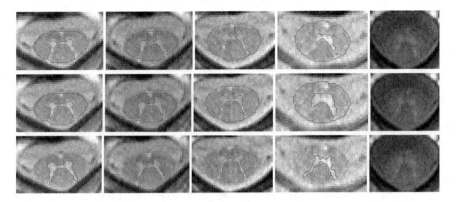

Fig. 3. *Upper row:* Solutions of (10) show disconnected GM regions and depend on the image quality. *Middle row:* Proposed solutions show anatomically consistent results. *Lower row:* GM contours of pixel-wise manual segmentations of rater 1.

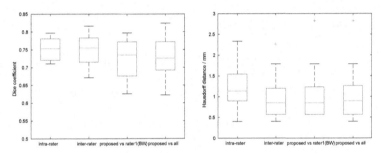

Fig. 4. GM segmentation results. *Dices:* intra-rater: binary vs grayscale; inter-rater: rater 1 vs 2 (grayscale); proposed vs rater 1 (binary); proposed (grayscale) vs rater 1 and 2 (binary and grayscale). *Hausdorff:* thresholded grayscale segmentations.

of the nearest neighbor $\hat{x}$. For the capacity function C we multiply the prior distance map with ζ. This way the boundary has more freedom in regions with high curvature, see Fig. 2.

It is an advantage to choose Δt_α smaller than 1 (we chose 0.2) because then the prior does not change too fast, in case the Chan-Vese solution at the initialization time has good quality and would be affected badly by the prior, which, in turn, would change the prior again.

4   Results

We implemented our models and algorithms in MATLAB and tested the GM results against the manual segmentation. For each dataset we created a statistical appearance model for (12) from the aligned manual segmentations of rater 1 and 2 of the remaining datasets, using principal component analysis. The CSF localization, spinal tract extraction and GM segmentation worked robustly and fully automatic on all 16 images. Figure 3 shows exemplary GM results. We notice that the CSF segmentation is not perfect, because the anterior median fissure is not seen in the first image, where the CSF has bright intensity and overrules the thin structure because of partial volume effects.

Figure 4 shows mean Dice coefficients (0.75) and average Hausdorff distances (1 mm) of the proposed GM results. The Hausdorff distances have the tendency to be large, because the thin-structured posterior horns are not always delineated with the same length. Taso et al. [13] reach mean GM Dice coefficients of 0.83. Since our image resolution and signal-to-noise ratio are low, our manual segmentation only reaches a mean intra- and inter-rater Dice of 0.75. Therefore we expect Dices at best in the latter range, when comparing our method to the manual raters. Hand-segmented results are thresholded with 0.6, because of the downsampling technique, and the automated results with a standard 0.5. The error for thresholding is in the range of non-thresholded inter-rater variance. The proposed automated solution therefore can be seen as a third rater.

5   Discussion and Conclusion

We developed a variational approach to segment GM inside the spinal cord on C3 level. The algorithm works robustly on the given data sets and achieves similar Dice and Hausdorff measures as hand-segmented results. The solutions of the algorithm depend more on the intensity values gathered through the MR sequence and less on prior knowledge. Prior knowledge is included but does not overrule the information given in the MR image.

The quality of the results depends strongly on the imaging quality because of the fine structures present in the GM. We expect better quality in new images and thus better segmentation results. The MR sequence is still experimental and further adaptations are necessary for use in clinical practice.

We consider to implement a spatially adaptive weighting factor between the information of a given MR image and of the prior knowledge. The simple ellipsoidal-shaped prior was only used to locate the CSF, and in the future CSF and WM appearance models will be included. Since variational algorithms can easily be extended to additional dimensions, our model can be adapted for 3D MR images with good WM/GM contrast.

References

1. Asman, A.J., Bryan, F.W., Smith, S.A., Reich, D.S., Landman, B.A.: Groupwise multi-atlas segmentation of the spinal cord's internal structure. Med. Image Anal. **18**(3), 460–471 (2014)
2. Aubert, G., Kornprobst, P.: The segmentation problem. Mathematical Problems in Image Processing. Applied Mathematical Sciences, vol. 147, pp. 153–187. Springer, New York (2002)
3. Boykov, Y.Y., Jolly, M.P.: Interactive graph cuts for optimal boundary & region segmentation of objects in N-D images. In: ICCV 2001, vol. 1, pp. 105–112 (2001)

4. Cremers, D., Schmidt, F.R., Barthel, F.: Shape priors in variational image segmentation: Convexity, Lipschitz continuity and globally optimal solutions. In: IEEE Conference on Computer Vision and Pattern Recognition, pp. 1–6 (2008)
5. De Leener, B., Taso, M., Cohen-Adad, J., Callot, V.: Segmentation of the human spinal cord. Magn. Reson. Mater. Phy. **29**(2), 125–153 (2016)
6. Grasmair, M., Lenzen, F.: Anisotropic total variation filtering. Appl. Math. Optim. **62**(3), 323–339 (2010)
7. Losseff, N.A., et al.: Spinal cord atrophy and disability in multiple sclerosis. A new reproducible and sensitive MRI method with potential to monitor disease progression. Brain J. Neurol. **119**(Pt 3), 701–708 (1996)
8. Olsson, C., Byröd, M., Overgaard, N.C., Kahl, F.: Extending continuous cuts: anisotropic metrics and expansion moves. In: ICCV 2009, pp. 405–412 (2009)
9. Overgaard, N.C., Fundana, K., Heyden, A.: Pose invariant shape prior segmentation using continuous cuts and gradient descent on lie groups. In: Tai, X.-C., Mørken, K., Lysaker, M., Lie, K.-A. (eds.) SSVM 2009. LNCS, vol. 5567, pp. 684–695. Springer, Heidelberg (2009). doi:10.1007/978-3-642-02256-2_57
10. Pezold, S., Horváth, A., Fundana, K., Tsagkas, C., Andělová, M., Weier, K., Amann, M., Cattin, P.C.: Automatic, robust, and globally optimal segmentation of tubular structures. In: Ourselin, S., Joskowicz, L., Sabuncu, M.R., Unal, G., Wells, W. (eds.) MICCAI 2016. LNCS, vol. 9902, pp. 362–370. Springer, Cham (2016). doi:10.1007/978-3-319-46726-9_42
11. Schlaeger, R., et al.: Spinal cord gray matter atrophy correlates with multiple sclerosis disability. Ann. Neurol. **76**(4), 568–580 (2014)
12. Tang, L., Wen, Y., Zhou, Z., von Deneen, K.M., Huang, D., Ma, L.: Reduced field-of-view DTI segmentation of cervical spine tissue. Magn. Reson. Imaging **31**(9), 1507–1514 (2013)
13. Taso, M., et al.: A reliable spatially normalized template of the human spinal cord – applications to automated white matter/gray matter segmentation and tensor-based morphometry (TBM) mapping of gray matter alterations occurring with age. NeuroImage **117**, 20–28 (2015)
14. Wang, X.F., Min, H., Zou, L., Zhang, Y.G.: A novel level set method for image segmentation by incorporating local statistical analysis and global similarity measurement. Pattern Recogn. **48**(1), 189–204 (2015)
15. Weigel, M., Bieri, O.: A simple and fast approach for spinal cord imaging at 3T with high in-plane resolution and good contrast. In: Proceedings of the 24th Annual Meeting of ISMRM, Singapore. p. 4408, May 2016
16. Yiannakas, M., Kearney, H., Samson, R., Chard, D., Ciccarelli, O., Miller, D., Wheeler-Kingshott, C.: Feasibility of grey matter and white matter segmentation of the upper cervical cord in vivo: a pilot study with application to magnetisation transfer measurements. NeuroImage **63**(3), 1054–1059 (2012)
17. Yuan, J., Bae, E., Tai, X.C.: A study on continuous max-flow and min-cut approaches. In: CVPR 2010, pp. 2217–2224 (2010)

Automated Intervertebral Disc Segmentation Using Deep Convolutional Neural Networks

Xing Ji[1], Guoyan Zheng[2], Daniel Belavy[3], and Dong Ni[1(✉)]

[1] School of Biomedical Engineering,
Shenzhen University, Shenzhen, China
nidong@szu.edu.cn
[2] Institute for Surgical Technology and Biomechanics,
University of Bern, Bern, Switzerland
guoyan.zheng@istb.unibe.ch
[3] Institute of Physical Activity and Nutrition Research,
Deakin University, Burwoodd, VIC, Australia

Abstract. In this paper, we propose to use deep convolutional neural networks to solve the challenging Intervertebral Disc (IVD) segmentation problem. We investigated the influence of four different patch sampling strategies on the performance of the deep convolutional neural networks. Evaluated on the MICCAI 2015 IVD segmentation challenge datasets, our method achieved a mean Dice overlap coefficient of 89.2% and a mean average absolute surface distance of 1.3 mm. The results achieved by our method are comparable with those achieved by the state-of-the-art methods.

1 Introduction

Intervertebral disc (IVD) degeneration is a major cause for chronic back pain and function incapacity [1]. Magnetic Resonance (MR) Imaging (MRI) has become one of the key investigative tools in clinical practice to image the spine with IVD degeneration, not only because MRI is non-invasive and does not use ionizing radiation, but more importantly because it offers good soft tissue contrast that allows for visualization of disc's internal structure [2].

MRI quantification has great potential as a tool for the diagnosis of disc pathology but before quantifying disc information, the IVDs need to be extracted from the MRI data. In the literature, different methods have been proposed for IVD segmentation [3–7]. There exist methods based on watershed algorithm [3], atlas registration [4], graph cuts with geometric priors from neighboring discs [5], template matching and statistical shape model [6], or anisotropic oriented flux detection [7]. All of these methods except [6] work only on 2D sagittal images.

Recently, machine learning-based methods have gained more and more interest. For example, Zhan et al. [8] presented a hierarchical strategy and local articulated model to detect vertebrae and discs from 3D MR images and Michael Kelm et al. [9] proposed to use iterated marginal space learning for spine detection in CT and MR images. A unified data-driven regression and classification

© Springer International Publishing AG 2016
J. Yao et al. (Eds.): CSI 2016, LNCS 10182, pp. 38–48, 2016.
DOI: 10.1007/978-3-319-55050-3_4

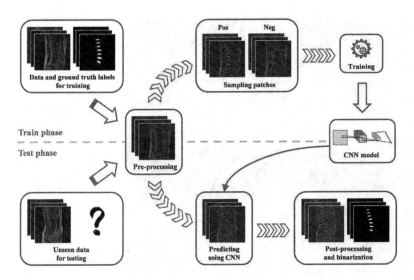

Fig. 1. A schematic view of the workflow for the present method. See main texts for details.

framework was suggested by Chen et al. [10] to tackle the problem of localization and segmentation of IVDs from T2-weighted MR data, and Wang et al. [11] proposed to address the segmentation of multiple anatomic structures in multiple anatomical planes from multiple imaging modalities via a sparse kernel machines-based regression.

The more recent development on deep neural networks, and in particular on convolutional neural networks (CNN), suggests another course of methods to solve the challenging IVD segmentation problem [12–16]. Contrary to conventional shallow learning methods where feature design is crucial, deep learning methods automatically learn hierarchies of relevant features directly from the training data [13]. Motivated by this development, we propose to use deep CNNs for the automated segmentation of IVDs from T2-weighted MRI data. Figure 1 shows a schematic view of the workflow for our method. Based on this workflow, we further investigate the influence of four different patch sampling strategies on the performance of the deep CNNs.

The paper is organized as follows. In Sect. 2, we will describe the proposed architecture and algorithm. The application to the MICCAI 2015 IVD segmentation challenge dataset will be presented in Sect. 3, and we conclude with a discussion in Sect. 4.

2 Methods

2.1 Data Description

The training data provided by the MICCAI 2015 IVD challenge organizers consist of 15 3D T2-weighted turbo spin echo MR images and the associated ground

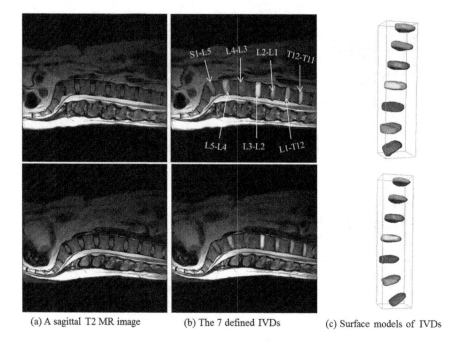

(a) A sagittal T2 MR image   (b) The 7 defined IVDs   (c) Surface models of IVDs

Fig. 2. Manual segmentation of 7 IVD regions from T2-weighted MR images.

truth segmentation (http://ijoint.istb.unibe.ch/challenge/index.html). These fifteen 3D T2-weighted MR images were acquired from fifteen patients in two different studies. Each patient was scanned with 1.5 Tesla MRI scanner of Siemens (Siemens Healthcare, Erlangen, Germany). The pixel spacings of all the images are sampled to $2 \times 1.25 \times 1.25\, mm^3$. There are 7 IVDs T11-L5 to be segmented from each image. Thus, in each image these IVD regions have been manually identified and segmented. Figure 2 shows two T2-weighted MR images and the segmented IVD regions from the images.

The MICCAI 2015 IVD challenge organizers also released two test datasets. Each test dataset consists of five 3D T2-weighted turbo spin echo MR images. Thus, in this paper, our CNNs are trained on the fifteen 3D training data first, and are then evaluated on the ten test data.

2.2 CNN Training

Pre-processing. For any 3D image either from the training data or from the test data, we conduct a pre-processing pipeline to define a region of interest (ROI). This is done for each sagittal slice in the 3D volume as follows: (1) we first downsample the slice to one fourth of the original size; (2) taking two pixels at the top-left corner and the top-right corner as two seed points respectively, we conduct region growing from each seed point with a pixel intensity threshold of 10, followed by a closing operation to get two regions that do not cover any

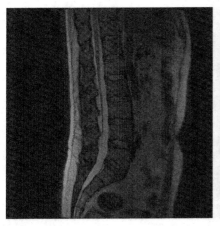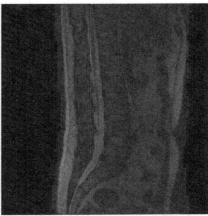

Fig. 3. A sagittal slice of a raw image (left) and the ROI after pre-processing (right, the red color-masked region is the ROI where we will work on). (Color figure online)

human tissue; (3) we finally upsample these two regions to the original image resolution and subtract the upsampled regions from the sagittal image space to get the ROI for later processing (training or testing). See Fig. 3 for an example.

Patch Sampling. Considering the relative small regions of interest for IVDs when compared with background region, we adopted following patch sampling strategy during the training stage:

- Voxels inside the IVDs. For each voxel inside the IVDs, we sample a patch around the voxel and assign the label of the sampled patch as 1 (a postive patch).
- Voxels at the boundary of the IVDs. In order to obtain the boundary of the IVDs, we first compute two label images. The first label image is obtained by dilating the ground truth label image with a $3 \times 3 \times 3$ structuring element and the second label image is obtained by eroding the ground truth label image with the same cubic structuring element as the first one. The boundary of the IVDs is then obtained by subtracting the second image from the first image. For each voxel at the boundary of the IVDs, we sample twice the same patch around the voxel. The patch label will be the same as the voxel label. Sampling these patches twice places more weight on the boundary voxels.
- The remaining voxels. We randomly sample negative patches from the remaining voxels in the ROI such that the number of the sampled negative patches is equal to the number of sampled positive patches.

Figure 4 shows a schematic view on how the sampling is done. We sample in total 1.6 million patches from the fifteen 3D T2 MR training data. Before we will use the sampled patches, we first compute an average patch from the sampled 1.6 million patches and then we subtract the average patch from the sampled patches to get zero-centered patches for training. In the test stage,

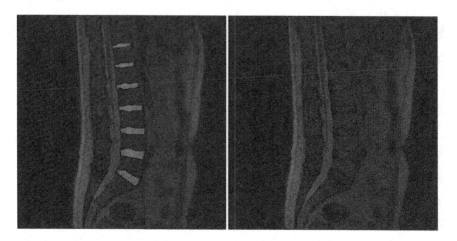

Fig. 4. Schematic view on a sagittal slice showing how the positive patches (left image, green color), the boundary patches (both left and right images, red color) and the negative patches (right image, green dots) are sampled (Color figure online)

for each sampled patch, we will also subtract the same average patch from the sampled patch.

Patch Design. We investigated two different types of patch. The first type of image patch is designed to be pure 2D image patches sampled from each sagittal slice of a 3D T2 MR image while the second type of image patch is designed to be 2.5D image patches sampled from three sequential sagittal slices of a 3D T2 MR image. For each type of patch, we investigated two different patch sizes, i.e., 20×20 vs. 32×32 pixels. In the remainder of this paper, these patch sampling strategy are referred to as: 2.5D20, 2D20, 2.5D32 and 2D32, respectively.

2.3 CNN Architecture

A CNN is a sequence of layers, and every layer of a CNN transforms one volume of activations to another through a differentiable function. We used four main types of layers to build our CNNs: Convolutional Layer (this is also where CNN derives its name), Max Pooling Layer, Fully-Connected Layer and the Output Layer (see Fig. 5 for details).

– Convolutional Layer. In the convolutional layer, a stack of feature maps will be produced by convolving the input with kernels, adding a bias term and finally applying a non-linear activation function. The activation function in our CNNs is chosen to be the retified linear unit (ReLU), which has been shown to expedite the training of CNN [13]. The depth of the stack of feature maps in our CNNs is chosen to be 128. Each of the feature maps is connected to all of the feature maps in the previous layer through filters of size 3×3 (Please note that this also applies to the first convolutional layer even when

2.5D patches are used. In such a case, each of the feature maps in the first convolutional layer is connected to all of the three input feature maps.). Both the stride size and the zero-padding size in our CNNs are chosen to be one pixel.

- Max Pooling Layer. In this layer, we will take each feature map output from the convolutional layer and perform a downsampling operation along the spatial dimensions. In our CNN, each unit in the pooling layer will output the maximum activation in the 2×2 input region. The stride size in this layer is chosen to be two pixels. Since this layer is used immediately after a convolutional layer, to easy the description, below we write these two layers as "Convolutional & Max Pooling Layers".

- Fully-Connected Layer. After several convolutional and max pooling layers, we will do high-level reasoning in this layer. Neurons in this layer have full connections to all activations in the previous layer.

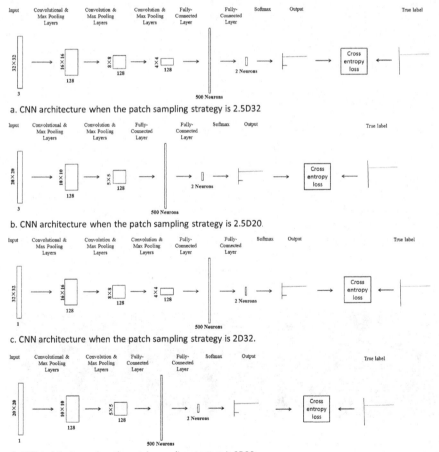

a. CNN architecture when the patch sampling strategy is 2.5D32

b. CNN architecture when the patch sampling strategy is 2.5D20.

c. CNN architecture when the patch sampling strategy is 2D32.

d. CNN architecture when the patch sampling strategy is 2D20.

Fig. 5. Schematic view of the architectures of our CNNs when different patch sampling strategies are used: a. 2.5D32; b. 2.5D20; c. 2D32; and d. 2D20.

– Output Layer. The output layer following the fully-connected layer has two outputs that correspond to the two tissue classes (IVD vs. background). A 2-way softmax layer is used to generate a distribution over the 2 class labels.

Figure 5a, b, c, and d illustrate the architecture of our CNNs when different patch sampling strategies are used. We have implemented our CNNs using Caffe [17] on a Linux system with two Nvidia K80 GPUs. Our network minimizes the cross entropy loss between the predicted label and the ground truth label. In addition, we use dropout [18] to avoid overfitting when training our CNNs, which sets the output of each neuron to zero with probability 0.5. We apply this technique to the first fully-connected layer of each CNN architecture in Fig. 5. The optimization of our CNNs was done using mini-batch stochastic gradient descent algorithm on the 1.6 million zero-centered training patches. We chose to use a batch size of 500. The learning rate was initially set to be 0.0001. In order to prevent overfitting, we set the weight decay to be 0.0005. During the training process, we monitored the change of the loss. As soon as the loss will not decrease any more, we drop the learning rate by a factor of 10. Such an adjustment was repeated twice. A CNN training was done when we reached the total number of iterations which was set to be 5000 or when the loss no longer decreased. It took on average about 20 min to finish the training of a CNN.

2.4 Voxel-Wise Inference and Post-processing

In the test stage, for each voxel in the ROI after pre-processing, we sample an image patch as the input to our trained CNNs. Output from any one of our trained CNNs is the probability of this voxel to be part of an IVD. After we computed probabilities of all voxels in the pre-processed ROI which we called the probability map, we utilized simple post-processing steps to get the final results. To this end, we first smoothed the probability map with a $5 \times 5 \times 5$ averaging filter. We then binarized the smoothed probability map using a threshold value of 0.5. Finally the segmentation mask was obtained by first conducting connected-component labeling to find disjoint areas and then removing those areas containing less than 512 voxels. We finally only kept the seven biggest

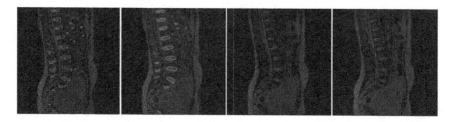

Fig. 6. Post-processing steps displayed on a 2D sagittal slice. Left: the probability map output from CNN; middle left: after smoothing; middle right: after threshold-based binarization; and right: output segmentation mask.

connected components counted from the bottom of the test image. Figure 6 shows details of the post-processing steps.

3   Experimental Results

3.1   Evaluation Metrics

The metrics introduced in the MICCAI 2015 IVD segmentation challenge are used here to evaluate the performance of our CNN. The evaluation metrics on IVD segmentation include the mean Dice overlap coefficients (MDOC) with standard deviation (SDDOC) between the ground truth segmentation and the automated segmentation, as well as the mean average absolute surface distance (MASD) with standard deviation (SDASD) between the surface models extracted from the ground truth segmentation and those extracted from the automated segmentation.

3.2   Segmentation Results

Table 1 shows the results of our method when evaluated on the Test1 dataset of the MICCAI 2015 IVD segmentation challenge and Table 2 shows the results of our method when evaluated on the Test2 dataset of the MICCAI 2015 IVD segmentation challenge. For both datasets, the best performance was obtained when 2D20 patch sampling strategy was used. With such a patch sampling strategy, we achieved a MDOC of 89.2% and a mean AAD of 1.26 mm. Furthermore, slightly better results were obtained when our method was evaluated on the

Table 1. Results on the Test1 dataset from the MICCAI 2015 IVD segmentation challenge when different patch sampling strategies are used

Image patch	MDOC (%)	SDDOC (%)	MASD (mm)	SDASD (mm)
2.5D20	88.7	3.4	1.30	0.17
2.5D32	79.2	7.5	1.56	0.19
2D20	89.2	3.0	1.27	0.17
2D32	86.6	4.6	1.36	0.22

Table 2. Results on the Test2 dataset from the MICCAI 2015 IVD segmentation challenge when different patch sampling strategies are used

Image patch	MDOC (%)	SDDOC (%)	MASD (mm)	SDASD (mm)
2.5D20	89.0	4.1	1.27	0.21
2.5D32	82.6	4.8	1.47	0.19
2D20	89.2	4.3	1.26	0.21
2D32	86.9	4.1	1.36	0.21

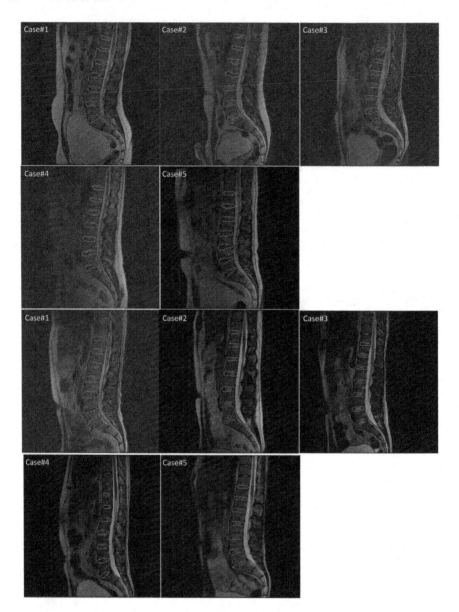

Fig. 7. Examples of segmentation visualized on 2D sagittal slices when 2D20 image patches were used. Top two rows: middle sagittal slices from the 5 3D images of the Test1 data; bottom two rows: middle sagittal slices from the 5 3D images of the Test2 data.

Test2 dataset than when our method was evaluated on the Test1 dataset. Without using any time-consuming registration step or incorporating any advanced shape prior, our method achieved results that were comparable with the state-of-the-art methods. For example, the best segmentation method in the MICCAI 2015 IVD segmentation challenge was the one submitted by Korez et al. [19] where a MDOC of 91.8% was reported. Other methods submitted to the same challenge achieved a MDOC in the range from 81.2% to 90.5% [20]. Figure 7 shows examples of automated segmentation of all ten test data. Although all the computations were done in 3D, we visualized the results on 2D sagittal slices.

It took our method on average 3 min to finish the inference of one 3D T2 test MR images.

4 Discussions

In this paper, we propose to use deep convolutional neural networks to solve the challenging IVD segmentation problem. The present method was evaluated on the MICCAI 2015 IVD segmentation challenge datasets and the results achieved by the present method were comparable with the state-of-the-art methods.

We investigated the influence of four different patch sampling strategies on the performance of our CNN. From our experimental results, it is interesting to find that the best performance was achieved when 2D20 image patches were used. Previous works in different application contexts have suggested both 2.5D [14,15] and 2D image patches [16]. Further work still need to be done to investigate why using 2.5D image patches did not achieved better results than using 2D image patches.

Acknowledgements. The paper is partially supported by the National Natural Science Funds of China (No. 61571304 and 81571758), and partially supported by the Swiss National Science Foundation Project No. 205321 − 157207/1. The acquisition of original images was supported by the Grant $14431/02/NL/SH2$ from the European Space Agency and grant 50WB0720 from the German Aerospace Center (DLR).

References

1. Modic, M., Ross, J.: Lumbar degenerative disk disease. Radiology **245**, 43–61 (2007)
2. Parizel, P., Goethem, J.V., Van den Hauwe, L., Voormolen, M.: Degenerative disc disease. In: Van Goethem, J.W.M., van den Hauwe, L., Parizel, P.M. (eds.) Spinal Imaging, pp. 127–156. Springer, Heidelberg (2007)
3. Chevrefils, C., Cheriet, F., Aubin, C.E., Grimard, G.: Texture analysis for automatic segmentation of intervertebral disks of scoliotic spines from MR images. IEEE Trans. Inf. Technol. Biomed. **13**, 608–620 (2009)
4. Michopoulou, S.K., Costaridou, L., Panagiotopoulos, E., Speller, R., Panayiotakis, G., Todd-Pokropek, A.: Atalas-based segmentation of degenerated lumbar intervertebral discs from MR images of the spine. IEEE Trans. Biomed. Eng. **56**(9), 2225–2231 (2009)
5. Ben, A.I., Punithakumar, K., Garvin, G., Romano, W., Li, S.: Graph cuts with invariant object-interaction priors: application to intervertebral disc segmentation. In: IPMI, pp. 221–232 (2011)

6. Neubert, A., Fripp, J., Shen, K., Salvado, O., Schwarz, R., Lauer, L., Engstrom, C., Crozier, S.: Automatic 3D segmentation of vertebral bodies and intervertebral discs from MRI. In: International Conference on Digitial Imaging Computing: Techniques and Applications (2011)

7. Law, M.W.K., Tay, K., Leung, A., Garvin, G.J., Li, S.: Intervertebral disc segmentation in MR images using anisotropic oriented flux. Med. Image Anal. **17**, 43–61 (2013)

8. Zhan, Y., Maneesh, D., Harder, M., Zhou, X.S.: Robust MR spine detection using hierarchical learning and local articulated model. In: Ayache, N., Delingette, H., Golland, P., Mori, K. (eds.) MICCAI 2012. LNCS, vol. 7510, pp. 141–148. Springer, Heidelberg (2012). doi:10.1007/978-3-642-33415-3_18

9. Michael Kelm, B., Wels, M., Zhou, S., Seifert, S., Suehling, M., Zheng, Y., Comaniciu, D.: Spine detection in CT and MR using iterated marginal space learning. Med. Image Anal. **17**(8), 1283–1292 (2013)

10. Chen, C., Belavy, D., Yu, W., Chu, C., Armbrecht, G., Bansmann, M., Felsenberg, D., Zheng, G.: Localization and segmentation of 3D intervertebral discs in MR images by data driven estimation. IEEE Trans. Med. Imaging **34**(8), 1719–1729 (2015)

11. Wang, Z., Zhen, X., Tay, K., et al.: Regression segmentation for M3 spinal images. IEEE Trans. Med. Imaging **34**(8), 1640–1648 (2015)

12. Bengio, Y.: Learning deep architectures for AI. Found. Trends Mach. Learn. **2**(1), 1–127 (2009)

13. Krizhevsky, A., Sutskever, I., Hinton, G.E.: Imagenet classification with deep convolutional neural networks. NIPS **2012**, 1097–1105 (2012)

14. Prasoon, A., Petersen, K., Igel, C., Lauze, F., Dam, E., Nielsen, M.: Deep feature learning for knee cartilage segmentation using a triplanar convolutional neural network. In: Mori, K., Sakuma, I., Sato, Y., Barillot, C., Navab, N. (eds.) MICCAI 2013. LNCS, vol. 8150, pp. 246–253. Springer, Heidelberg (2013). doi:10.1007/ 978-3-642-40763-5_31

15. Roth, H.R., Lu, L., Seff, A., Cherry, K.M., Hoffman, J., Wang, S., Liu, J., Turkbey, E., Summers, R.M.: A new 2.5D representation for lymph node detection using random sets of deep convolutional neural network observations. In: Golland, P., Hata, N., Barillot, C., Hornegger, J., Howe, R. (eds.) MICCAI 2014. LNCS, vol. 8673, pp. 520–527. Springer, Cham (2014). doi:10.1007/978-3-319-10404-1_65

16. Roth, H.R., Yao, J., Lu, L., et al.: Detection of sclerotic spine metastases via random aggregation of deep convolutional neural network classifications. In: Recent Advances in Computational Methods and Clinical Applications for Spine, Imaging, pp. 3–12 (2015)

17. Jia, Y., Shelhamer, E., et al.: Caffe: convolutional architecture for fast feature embedding. arXiv preprint arXiv:1408.5093 (2014)

18. Hinton, G.E., Srivastava, N., et al.: Improving neural networks by preventing coadaption of feature detectors. arXiv preprint arXiv:1207.0580.5

19. Korez, R., Ibragimov, B., Likar, B., Pernuš, F., Vrtovec, T.: Deformable model-based segmentation of intervertebral discs from MR spine images by using the SSC descriptor. In: Vrtovec, T., Yao, J., Glocker, B., Klinder, T., Frangi, A., Zheng, G., Li, S. (eds.) CSI 2015. LNCS, vol. 9402, pp. 117–124. Springer, Cham (2016). doi:10.1007/978-3-319-41827-8_11

20. Vrtovec, T., Yao, J., Glocker, B., Klinder, T., Frangi, A., Zheng, G., Li, S. (eds.): CSI 2015. LNCS, vol. 9402. Springer, Cham (2016)

Localization

Fully Automatic Localisation of Vertebrae in CT Images Using Random Forest Regression Voting

Paul A. Bromiley[1](✉), Eleni P. Kariki[2], Judith E. Adams[2], and Timothy F. Cootes[1]

[1] Centre for Imaging Sciences, University of Manchester, Manchester, UK
{paul.bromiley,timothy.f.cootes}@manchester.ac.uk
[2] Radiology and Manchester Academic Health Science Centre, Central Manchester University Hospitals NHS Foundation Trust, Manchester, UK
eleni.kariki@cmft.nhs.uk, judith.adams@manchester.ac.uk

Abstract. We describe a system for fully automatic vertebra localisation and segmentation in 3D CT volumes containing arbitrary regions of the spine, with the aim of detecting osteoporotic fractures. To avoid the difficulties of high-resolution manual annotation on overlapping structures in 3D, the system consists of several 2D operations. First, a Random Forest regressor is used to localise the spinal midplane in a coronal maximum intensity projection. A 2D sagittal image showing the midplane is then produced. A second set of regressors are used to localise each vertebral body in this image. Finally, a Random Forest Regression Voting Constrained Local Model is used to segment each detected vertebra.

The system was evaluated on 402 CT volumes. 83% of vertebrae between T4 and L4 were detected and, of these, 97% were segmented with a mean error of less than or equal to $1\,mm$. A simple classifier was applied to perform a fracture/non-fracture classification for each image, achieving 69% recall at 70% precision.

1 Introduction

Osteoporosis is a common skeletal disorder characterised by a reduction in bone mineral density (BMD). This is commonly assessed using dual energy X-ray absorptiometry (DXA); a T-score of $<$-2.5 (i.e. more than 2.5 standard deviations below the mean in young adults) [13] is used as a criterion suggesting osteoporosis. It significantly increases the risk of fractures, most commonly occurring in the hip, wrist or vertebrae. Approximately 40% of postmenopausal Caucasian women are affected, increasing their lifetime risk of fragility fractures to as much as 40% [13]. Osteoporosis therefore presents a significant public health problem for an ageing population. However, between 30%–60% of vertebral fractures may be asymptomatic and only about one third of those present on images come to clinical attention; they are frequently not reported by radiologists, not entered

© Springer International Publishing AG 2016
J. Yao et al. (Eds.): CSI 2016, LNCS 10182, pp. 51–63, 2016.
DOI: 10.1007/978-3-319-55050-3_5

into medical records, and do not lead to preventative treatments [8]. Many of these cases involve images acquired for purposes other than assessment for the presence of vertebral fractures, so identification may be opportunistic. However, a recent multi-centre, multinational prospective study [9] found a false negative rate of 34% for reporting vertebral fractures from lateral radiographs of the thoracolumbar spine. The potential utility of computer-aided vertebral fracture identification systems is therefore considerable. Modern clinical imaging is primarily digital, with images acquired in Digital Imaging and Communications in Medicine (DICOM) format and stored on a Picture Archiving and Communication System (PACS). A system that could query a PACS to extract images that include the spine, automatically segment vertebrae, detect any abnormal shape, and report suspect images for further investigation by a radiologist, would therefore be particularly valuable.

CT is arguably the ideal modality for opportunistic osteoporotic vertebral fracture identification, due to the large number of procedures (4.3 million per year within the UK National Health Service [12]) and the high image quality. However, a recent audit at the Manchester Royal Infirmary revealed that only 13% of such fractures visible on CT images were identified [15], similar to identification rates reported in the literature [1]. Proposed reasons for such low rates [1] include the difficulty of identifying vertebral height reduction on axial images. Routine production of coronal and/or sagittal reformatted images has been proposed, and is being adopted, but reporting rates on such images remain low [1].

We describe a system for fully automatic localisation and segmentation of vertebrae in sagittal reformatted CT image volumes covering arbitrary regions of the spine, based on landmark point annotation. Manual annotation on 3D spinal images for model training would be a challenging task, due to the large number of points required to quantify vertebral shape accurately. Therefore, several 2D operations are used. A coronal maximum intensity projection (MIP) of the volume is produced, highlighting the bony structures. Random Forest (RF) Regression Voting (RFRV) is used to localise points on the spine. This takes advantage of the fact that the patient is supine in the CT scanner, and so is not subject to arbitrary rotation in the axial image plane. A single, thick-slice, 2D sagittal image is then produced, showing the midplanes of all vertebrae present. A second set of RF regressors is used to localise the posterior-inferior vertebral corners in this image. Both of these initialisation stages are based on the algorithm described in [4]. Finally, the vertebral corner points are used to initialise a Random Forest Regression Voting Constrained Local Model (RFRV-CLM), based on [3], which provides a high-resolution segmentation of the vertebrae allowing subsequent shape measurement. These algorithms are described briefly in Sect. 2. The reader is referred to [3,4] for a more complete description, and discussion of related literature.

2   Method

2.1   Random Forest Regression Voting

Random Forest Regression Voting (RFRV) uses a RF [2] regressor to localise a landmark, trained to predict the offset to that point based on local patches of image features. The training data consists of a set of images $\mathbf{I}$ with manual annotations $\mathbf{x}_l$ of the point on each. Random displacements $\mathbf{d}_j$ are generated by sampling from a uniform distribution with apothem d_{max} and the same dimensionality as the images. Image patches of area w_{patch}^2 are extracted at these displacements from $\mathbf{x}_l$ in each training image, and features $\mathbf{f}_j$ are derived from them. Haar-like features [14] are used, as they have proven effective for a range of applications and can be calculated efficiently from integral images. To allow for inaccurate initial estimates of pose during model fitting, and to make the detector locally pose-invariant, the process is repeated with random perturbations in scale and orientation. A RF is then constructed; each tree is trained on a bootstrap sample of pairs $\{(\mathbf{f}_j, \mathbf{d}_j)\}$ from the training data using a standard, greedy approach. At each node, a random set of n_{feat} features is chosen, and a feature f_i and threshold t that best split the data into two compact groups are selected by minimising an entropy measure [11]. The process is terminated at a maximum depth D_{max} or minimum number of samples N_{min}, and repeated to generate a forest of n_{trees}.

2.2   RFRV Initialiser Fitting

The coronal and sagittal initialisation algorithms used here are based on [4], and use RF regressors trained as described in Sect. 2.1. An exhaustive search is performed over a query image, by defining a grid of positions with a spacing of 3 pixels. The RFs are applied at each position, and give predictions of the displacement to the landmarks. The search is repeated at a range of angle and scale variation: -0.8 to 0.8 radians in steps of $\theta_r = 0.1$, and scales from 0.1 to 4 in rational/integer steps. The predicted landmark locations from each tree are collected in a Hough-style voting array. An RF trained to localise a point on a specific vertebral level will respond strongly to the equivalent points on neighbouring vertebrae, due to their similar shapes, predicting the closest to each search position. Full coverage of the spine can be achieved by training a single RF on concatenated data $\{(\mathbf{f}_j, \mathbf{d}_j)\}$ from multiple levels. Alternatively, RFs can be trained on each level and applied in parallel, voting into a single array. The array is then smoothed using a Gaussian kernel of standard deviation twice the resolution of the search grid, allowing detection of modes using nineway maximum. Modes with weights lower than 20% of the strongest response are discarded. (In contrast to [4], no additional weighting of the modes was used here). A graphical method is then used to extract an ordered, linked set of modes, representing landmarks on all visible vertebra, and to discard false detections. Starting from the strongest mode, an iterative search is performed in the local inferior and superior directions, determined from the average pose of the RFRV detections for that mode. At each iteration, the closest mode within an angle constraint of $\theta_t = 2\theta_r$ is added to the set, terminating when no further modes meet the constraint.

2.3 Constrained Local Models (CLMs)

The CLM [7] uses a statistical shape model (SSM) to constrain the fitting of multiple, independent RFRVs for a set of landmarks. The training data consists of a set of images $\mathbf{I}$ with manual annotations $\mathbf{x}_l$ of a set of N points $l = 1...N$ on each. The images are first aligned into a standardised reference frame using a similarity registration, giving a transformation T with parameters θ, and then resampled into this frame by applying $\mathbf{I}_r(m, n) = \mathbf{I}(T_\theta^{-1}(m, n))$, where (m, n) specify pixel coordinates. The reference frame width, in pixels, is controlled by a parameter w_{frame}, allowing variation of the resolution of the resampled images. The concatenated, reference-frame coordinates of the points in each training image define its shape; the SSM is generated by applying principal component analysis (PCA) to the set of training shapes [5]. This yields a linear model of shape variation, giving the position of point l

$$\mathbf{x}_l = T_\theta(\bar{\mathbf{x}}_l + \mathbf{P}_l\mathbf{b} + \mathbf{r}_l) \tag{1}$$

where $\bar{\mathbf{x}}_l$ is the mean point position in the reference frame, $\mathbf{P}_l$ is a set of modes of variation, $\mathbf{b}$ encodes the shape model parameters, and $\mathbf{r}_l$ allows small deviations from the model. For each point $l = 1...N$, an RF R_l is trained as described in Sect. 2.1, using data from the resampled images.

2.4 RFRV-CLM Fitting

The fitting of a RFRV-CLM to a query image $\mathbf{I}_q$ is initialised via an estimate of pose ($\mathbf{b}$ and θ) from a previous model or a manual initialisation. The image is resampled in the reference frame using the current pose $\mathbf{I}_{qr}(m, n) = \mathbf{I}_q(T_\theta^{-1}(m, n))$. For each point l, a grid of locations $\mathbf{z}_l$ is defined covering a search range of apothem d_{search} around the initial estimate of its position. Regressor R_l is applied to the image features extracted from the local patch around each grid location. Each tree in R_l predicts the offset to the true point position, and casts a vote into an accumulator array C_l at the predicted position. This is performed independently for each point. The shape model places a constraint on the results from all regressors. The quality of fit Q is given by

$$Q(\mathbf{p}) = \Sigma_{l=1}^{N} C_l(T_\theta(\bar{\mathbf{x}}_l + \mathbf{P}_l\mathbf{b} + \mathbf{r}_l)) \;\; \text{s.t.} \;\; \mathbf{b}^T\mathbf{S}_b^{-1}\mathbf{b} \leq M_t \;\; \text{and} \;\; |\mathbf{r}_l| < r_t \tag{2}$$

where $\mathbf{S}_b$ is the covariance matrix of shape model parameters $\mathbf{b}$, M_t is a threshold on the Mahalanobis distance, and r_t is a threshold on the residuals. M_t is chosen using the cumulative distribution function (CDF) of the χ^2 distribution so that 98% of samples from a multivariate Gaussian of the appropriate dimension would fall within it. This ensures a plausible shape by assuming a flat distribution for model parameters $\mathbf{b}$ constrained within hyper-ellipsoidal bounds [6]. Q is iteratively optimised, over parameters $\mathbf{p} = \{\mathbf{b}, \theta, \mathbf{r}_l\}$, as described in [11].

2.5   Data Collection and Manual Annotation

The PACS (Centricity Universal Viewer, GE Healthcare, Little Chalford, Buckinghamshire, UK) at Central Manchester University Hospital NHS Trust (CMFT) was queried to produce a list of CT scans acquired during May and June 2014 and January to September 2015. The scans that (a) were from non-trauma patients, (b) included any part of the thoracic or lumbar spine and (c) were of patients over 18 years of age, were selected. This gave a list of 868 patients' scans. The CMFT PACS was also queried for non-trauma CT scans during January to April and July to December 2014 in patients over 60 years of age that contained osteoporotic vertebral fractures, producing a second list of 132 patients. The sagittal reformatted volumes from both lists were downloaded in DICOM format. 402 volumes were selected to form a training set for the models, including the 132 fracture-rich images to ensure high fracture prevalence. The remaining images were reserved for validation purposes. The 402 image list was divided into quarters for leave-1/4-out training and testing, with the fracture-rich images distributed evenly. Each volume was up-sampled to give isotropic voxel dimensions, equal to the smallest voxel dimension from the original volume, using tri-cubic interpolation.

A coronal MIP was generated from each image volume, and manual annotation of a landmark on the neural arch of each visible vertebra was performed. 2D sagittal images were generated from each volume, as described Sect. 2.6, by summing all sagittal slice rasters within ±5 mm of the plane defined by the coronal annotations. This thickness was chosen by manual inspection of the results, to minimise blurring of the endplates whilst ensuring that the middle of each endplate was visible. High-resolution manual annotation of 33 points on each vertebral body between T4 and L4 inclusive was then performed on the sagittal images by trained radiographers. Finally, each annotated vertebra was classified by an expert radiologist as normal, deformed but not fractured, or grade 1, 2 or 3 osteoporotic fracture, according to the Genant definitions [10].

2.6   Midplane Image Extraction

Osteoporotic vertebral fractures typically develop as a depression of the middle of the vertebral endplates (biconcave fracture), followed by anterior collapse of the vertebral body (wedge fracture) and posterior collapse (crush fracture). Therefore, height reductions must be measured at the endplate midplanes to avoid underestimation of the fracture severity. If the superior-inferior axis of the subject is not aligned exactly with the CT scanner, or if any degree of scoliosis is present, then no single slice of the sagittal reformatted volume will pass through all midplanes. Therefore, an algorithm was developed to extract a 2D image along the spine midplane. First, a coronal maximum intensity projection (MIP) was produced from the volume, to show the bony structures. In particular, the point at which the laminae join to form the spinous process of the neural arch is a distinctive, U-shaped structure on each vertebra in such images (Fig. 1a). These points were manually annotated on each image (see Sect. 2.5).

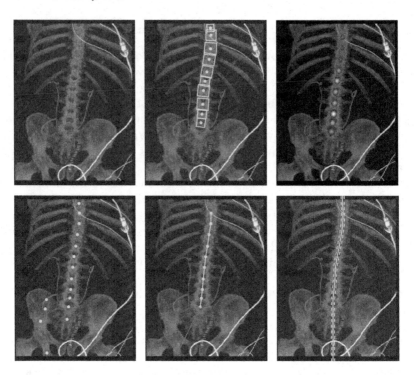

Fig. 1. (Top left) An example coronal MIP of a CT volume; note the presence of confounding structures both outside (cardiac monitoring equipment) and inside (from previous abdominal surgery) the subject. (Top centre) Manual annotations of the neural arch, with the undisplaced sample regions used in RF training. (Top right) Density plot of the Hough voting array from the RF search. (Bottom left) Modes of the array. (Bottom centre) Result of linking and filtering; red links are those rejected by the filter. (Bottom right) Extrapolated piecewise-linear curve through the filtered modes (solid line) and the $\pm 5\,mm$ range (dashed line) over which sagittal rasters were summed to produce the sagittal projection. (Color figure online)

A RF regressor was then trained to localise the neural arch points as described in Sect. 2.1. Undisplaced sample patches were defined by using half of the average vector to the neighbouring points as the apothem of a square region of interest (ROI) (Fig. 1b). Free parameters were set to the values given in [4], and a single RFRV was trained using data from all points. Example images of each stage of the algorithm are shown in Fig. 1. Several confounding structures are visible inside and outside the body. The algorithm was robust to such features, but did produce false detections on some non-spine bony structures, such as the pelvis and mandible. Therefore, a filtering stage was implemented. Any image with fewer than four detections was removed from the analysis. The median L_m of the distances between neighbouring modes was then calculated. If the first or last mode in the list was further than $3L_m$ from its neighbour, it was removed.

The final set of ordered, filtered modes defined a midplane through the volume, and was used to extract a 2D sagittal image. A piecewise-linear curve was defined through the modes; at the extremities, it was extrapolated vertically to the boundary of the volume (Fig. 1f). For each axial slice from the original volume, all anteroposterior raster lines (i.e. rasters of sagittal slices) that passed within D_t of this curve were averaged to give a single raster line of a sagittal image. Repeating this for all axial images gave a single, thick-slice, 2D sagittal image that showed the midplane of each vertebra, but remained in the coordinate system of the original volume, so points annotated onto it could be directly translated to projections of a different D_t. In the remainder of this paper, "manual" and "automatic" projection refer to images produced from the manual and automatic annotations on the coronal MIP images, respectively.

2.7   Vertebra Localisation

Next, a set of RF regressors was trained to detect the inferior corners of each vertebral body present in the sagittal projection images. Manual annotations of the vertebrae from T4 to L4 were performed as described in Sect. 2.5 (Fig. 2a). As in [4], undisplaced sample patches were defined as square ROIs with the two lower endplate corner points at proportional positions of $(0.25, 0.75)$ and $(0.75, 0.75)$ (Fig. 2b). One RF regressor was trained for each vertebral level from T5 to L3, using only images where both neighbors were present, to prevent strong responses to the boundaries of the image volume.

Fitting and extraction of a linked set of modes $\mathbf{x}_l$, $l = 1...n_m$ proceeded as described in Sect. 2.6 (Fig. 2). The aim was to use the detected vertebral corners to initialise an RFRV-CLM that modeled a triplet of neighbouring vertebrae, so it was essential to deal with any missing detections. Therefore, several filters were applied. First, all images with fewer than three detections were discarded, as they could not provide a reliable initialisation. In each image, the distance between neighbouring modes was compared to the median distance between all pairs of neighbours. Where the ratio was greater than 1.5, the most probable number of missed detections n_l was

$$n_l = \left\lfloor \frac{L_l}{\mu_{1/2}(L)} + 0.5 \right\rfloor - 1 \quad \text{where} \quad L = \{L_l \,|\, L_l = ||\mathbf{x}_{l+1} - \mathbf{x}_l|| \; \forall i \in \{1, n_m - 1\}\}$$

(3)

where $\mu_{1/2}(.)$ represents the median, and n_l points $(0.0, 0.0)$ were entered into the list to represent missing detections. Where this left a singlet or doublet of modes at the end of the list, these were removed. Finally, all modes outside the range of the detections from the coronal initialisation (Fig. 2c) were removed.

2.8   High-Resolution Vertebral Segmentation

Finally, a high-resolution segmentation of the vertebrae detected by the sagittal initialisation algorithm was performed using an RFRV-CLM (see Sects. 2.3 and 2.4). The model used a 2-stage, coarse-to-fine RFRV-CLM covering a triplet

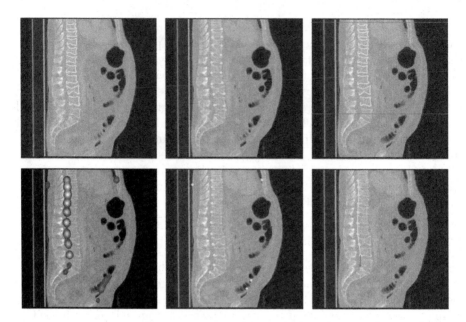

Fig. 2. (Top left) An example ±5 mm manual sagittal image projection from a CT volume, with high-resolution manual annotation. (Top centre) Inferior corner points, used to define sampling ROIs for RF training. (Top right) ±5 mm automatic sagittal image projection, with the manual annotations superimposed; the red lines show the extent of the RFRV annotations on the coronal maximum intensity projection. (Bottom left) Smoothed Hough voting array of the posterior-inferior corner point regressors. •(Bottom centre) Modes of the Hough voting array, detected using a nine-way maximum. (Bottom right) Result of linking and filtering; red points are those rejected by the filters. (Color figure online)

of vertebrae with 33 points on each. It was trained on all triplets of vertebrae from the training images. All free parameters were set to the values given in [3]. Fitting was initialised using the filtered list of posterior-inferior corner points from the sagittal regressor described in Sect. 2.7. All points represented as $(0.0, 0.0)$ were considered to be undefined. The model was fitted to all triplets of neighbouring vertebrae with at least two defined points. Points from the fitted models were then concatenated to give the final segmentation (Fig. 5a). Averaging was not applied; where two models covered a single vertebra, points from the central vertebra in a triplet were used in preference to those from an extremal vertebra, and only points on vertebrae with a defined initialisation point were used.

3 Evaluation

Training and testing of the system on the 402 images was performed in a leave-1/4-out fashion. Errors for the coronal initialisation were measured as the mean of the minimum Euclidean distances, over each image, between the detected

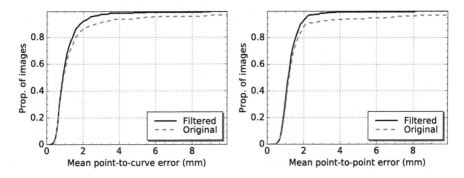

Fig. 3. Cumulative distribution functions showing the accuracy of the coronal and sagittal initialisation algorithms, before and after filtering. (Left) The mean P2C error of points on the spine midline in each image produced by the coronal regressors. (Right) The mean P2P error of posterior-inferior vertebral corner points in each image produced by the sagittal regressors.

points and a piecewise linear curve through the manual annotations (P2C error). For the sagittal initialisation, they were measured as the mean of the Euclidean distance, over each image, between the detected points and the closest manually annotated posterior-inferior vertebral corner point (P2P error). In both cases, detections outside the axial range of the manual annotations, $\pm$half of the median vertebra height, were removed from the analysis to avoid penalising accurate detections of vertebra that had not been manually annotated.

Figure 3 shows CDFs of the coronal initialisation errors. Prior to filtering, 94.3% of the midplanes had a mean error of $\leq 5\,mm$, and this rose to 98.3% after filtering. The difference at $\leq 10\,mm$ was small (98.3% and 99.2%). Therefore, as with the manual projections, a thickness of $D_t = \pm 5\,mm$ was used for automatic sagittal projection[1]. The filtering removed 41 images (10.2%). Figure 3 also shows CDFs of the sagittal initialisation errors. The mean errors across all points in all images were 2.14 mm prior to filtering, and 1.34 mm after; the medians were 0.98 mm and 0.96 mm, respectively. At the higher end of the CDF, 97.5% of all points in all images achieved $\leq 5\,mm$ prior to filtering, rising to 99.4% after filtering. The filtering removed 27 images from the analysis i.e. 6.7%, for a total of 16.9% removed during both initialisation stages.

An example of RFRV-CLM annotation on an automatically projected image with automatic sagittal initialisation is shown in Fig. 5a. Again, any vertebrae where the centroid lay outside the axial range of the manually annotated vertebrae, $\pm$half of the median vertebral height, were eliminated from the analysis. The error for each vertebra was then calculated as the mean of the minimum Euclidean distances between each automatic annotation and a piecewise-linear curve through the manual annotations (P2C error). Correspondence between

---

[1] The remainder of the evaluation was repeated with $D_t = \pm 10\,mm$, but this produced no improvements in the accuracy of subsequent stages, and the results are not reported here.

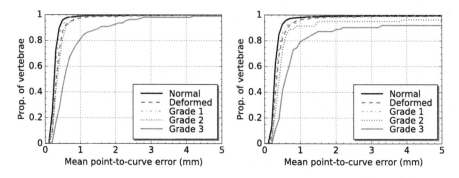

Fig. 4. Cumulative distribution functions of P2C error for high-resolution annotations on vertebrae using manual (left) and automatic (right) coronal and sagittal initialisation, divided by vertebral classification.

Table 1. Statistics of the mean point-to-curve errors on each vertebra after RFRV-CLM fitting, using manual and automatic initialisation.

Diagnosis	% of Sample	Manual initialisation		Automatic initialisation		
		Median (mm)	$\% > 2\,mm$	% Detected	Median (mm)	$\% > 2\,mm$
Normal	64.7%	0.24	0.55%	84.7%	0.27	0.83%
Deformed	25.2%	0.30	1.29%	84.9%	0.32	1.51%
Grade 1	2.84%	0.27	0.00%	75.0%	0.30	0.00%
Grade 2	3.71%	0.34	0.68%	71.3%	0.41	4.87%
Grade 3	3.59%	0.56	7.27%	56.8%	0.57	11.11%

automatically and manually annotated vertebrae was established by calculating this error for all manual vertebrae, and taking the smallest response. Figure 4 shows CDFs of these errors for both the fully automatic system, and for RFRV-CLM fits to manual sagittal projections, initialised using manual annotations on the vertebral corners. Numerical data derived from these curves, together with the percentages of all vertebrae between T4 and L4 detected (including those in images discarded during the initialisation stages) are given in Table 1, using a mean error of $\geq 2\,mm$ to indicate fit failure. The results show that automatic coronal and sagittal initialisation had little effect on the accuracy of successful RFRV-CLM fits. However, they did lead to a 4 percentage point rise in fit failures on moderate and severe fractures. Overall, 67.2% of the fractured vertebrae were detected by the fully automatic system, of which 89.1% were successfully fitted according to the $\geq 2\,mm$ threshold.

The significance of the segmentation accuracy was evaluated by applying a simple classifier, based on six-point morphometry, as described in [3]. The anterior h_a, middle h_m and posterior h_p heights of each detected vertebra were calculated from the relevant points, together with a predicted posterior height $h_{p'}$, calculated as the maximum of the posterior heights of the four closest vertebrae. The wedge $r_w = h_a/h_p$, biconcavity $r_b = h_m/h_p$, and crush $r_c = h_p/h_{p'}$

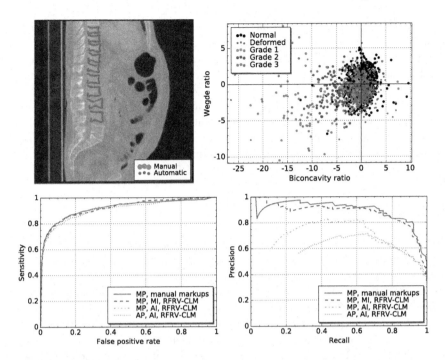

Fig. 5. (Top left) Example RFRV-CLM fit based on automatic coronal and sagittal initialisation. (Top right) Biconcavity and wedge ratios for all detected vertebrae. (Bottom left) ROC curves for classification of vertebrae, based on 6-point morphometry, for manual annotations and RFRV-CLM fits with stages of manual and automatic projection (MP and AP, respectively) and initialisation (MI and AI, respectively). (Bottom right) Precision-recall curves for classification of images.

ratios were derived, and the data were whitened by subtracting the medians of each ratio and dividing by the square-root of the covariance matrix, calculated using the median standard deviation. The data contained far more normal than deformed or fractured vertebrae, and so this process whitened to the distribution of the normal class. A scatter plot of r_b and r_w for all detected vertebrae between T4 and L4 is shown in Fig. 5b. A simple fracture/non-fracture classification was performed by applying a threshold to $r_c^2 + r_b^2 + r_w^2$; deformed vertebrae were counted correct when classified into either class. This was applied to the manual annotations, the RFRV-CLM fits on manually projected images initialised from both manual and automatic corner points, and to the fully automatic system. Receiver-operator characteristic (ROC) curves produced by varying the threshold are shown in Fig. 5d. The classifier achieved 80% sensitivity at a 10% false positive rate. More importantly, however, the fully automatic system achieved sensitivities no worse than 2% points lower than classification from manual projection and annotation, at any threshold.

The classifier was also applied on a per-image basis. This simulated the use of the system in clinical practice, as described in Sect. 1, to generate a list of potentially fracture-containing images. A threshold on $r_c^2 + r_b^2 + r_w^2$ was used to classify each automatically detected vertebra, and classify the images into two groups: all vertebrae normal; some vertebrae fractured. Images filtered out during initialisation were classified as fractured. Manual diagnoses were used to classify the images into normal and fractured groups, counting non-fracture deformities as normal. Figure 5d shows precision-recall curves produced by varying the threshold. Note that curves for automatic initialisation do not reach $(0, 1)$, due to the filtered images being classified as fractured. The fully automatic system achieved 69% recall (higher than current clinical practice; see Sect. 1) at 70% precision (i.e. 2/3 of reported images contained fractures).

4   Conclusion

The strikingly low detection rates for osteoporotic vertebral fractures on CT image volumes in clinical practice create an opportunity for an automatic system that can draw attention to images containing fractured vertebrae. The high image quality and 3D nature of CT volumes allow the automatic extraction of a single, thick, 2D sagittal slice that shows the vertebral midplanes, and does not suffer the problems of overlapping bony structures (ribs, scapulae and iliac crests) that make accurate vertebral segmentation difficult in alternative modalities such as DXA. Robust and accurate segmentation can then be achieved using a RFRV-CLM, allowing quantification of vertebral shape. This paper has shown that, even using a simple classifier, detection rates can be achieved that exceed those found in clinical practice. In future work, we intend to investigate the use of more accurate classifiers. The shape parameters of the SSM that forms part of the RFRV-CLM would provide a more complete quantification of vertebral shape than the six-point morphometry approach described above. However, osteoporosis also changes the texture of bone, since it affects horizontal trabeculae more than vertical ones. Therefore, classifiers based on both shape and texture will also be investigated.

Acknowledgment. This publication presents independent research supported by the Health Innovation Challenge Fund (grant no. HICF-R7-414/WT100936), a parallel funding partnership between the Department of Health and Wellcome Trust. The views expressed in this publication are those of the authors and not necessarily those of the Department of Health or Wellcome Trust. The authors acknowledge the invaluable assistance of Mrs Chrissie Alsop, Mr Stephen Capener, Mrs Imelda Hodgkinson, Mr Michael Machin, and Mrs Sue Roberts, who performed the manual annotations.

References

1. Adams, J.E.: Opportunistic identification of vertebral fractures. J. Clin. Densitometry **19**(1), 54–62 (2016)
2. Breiman, L.: Random forests. Mach. Learn. **45**, 5–32 (2001)

3. Bromiley, P.A., Adams, J.E., Cootes, T.F.: Localisation of vertebrae on DXA images using constrained local models with random forest regression voting. In: Yao, J., Glocker, B., Klinder, T., Li, S. (eds.) Recent Advances in Computational Methods and Clinical Applications for Spine Imaging. Lecture Notes in Computational Vision and Biomechanics, vol. 20, pp. 156–172. Springer, Cham (2015)

4. Bromiley, P.A., Adams, J.E., Cootes, T.F.: Automatic localisation of vertebrae in DXA images using random forest regression voting. In: Vrtovec, T., Yao, J., Glocker, B., Klinder, T., Frangi, A., Zheng, G., Li, S. (eds.) CSI 2015. LNCS, vol. 9402, pp. 38–51. Springer, Cham (2016). doi:10.1007/978-3-319-41827-8_4

5. Cootes, T.F., Edwards, G.J., Taylor, C.J.: Active appearance models. IEEE TPAMI **23**, 681–685 (2001)

6. Cootes, T.F., Taylor, C.J., Cooper, D.H., Graham, J.: Active shape models - their training and application. Comput. Vis. Image Und. **61**(1), 38–59 (1995)

7. Cristinacce, D., Cootes, T.: Automatic feature localisation with constrained local models. Pattern Recogn. **41**(10), 3054–3067 (2008)

8. Cummings, S.R., Melton, J.: Epidemiology and outcomes of osteoporotic fractures. Lancet **359**(9319), 1761–1767 (2002)

9. Delmas, P.D., van de Langerijt, L., Watts, N.B., Eastell, R., Genant, H.K., Grauer, A., Cahall, D.L.: Underdiagnosis of vertebral fractures is a worldwide problem: the IMPACT study. J. Bone Miner. Res. **20**(4), 557–563 (2005)

10. Genant, H.K., Wu, C.Y., Kuijk, C.V., Nevitt, M.C.: Vertebral fracture assessment using a semi-quantitative technique. J. Bone Miner. Res. **8**(9), 1137–1148 (1993)

11. Lindner, C., Bromiley, P.A., Ionita, M., Cootes, T.F.: Robust and accurate shape model matching using random forest regression-voting. IEEE TPAMI **37**(9), 1862–1874 (2015)

12. Operational Information for Commissioning: Diagnostic imaging dataset statistical release. Technical report, NHS, UK, May 2016. www.england.nhs.uk/statistics/wp-content/uploads/sites/2/2015/08/Provisional-Monthly-Diagnostic-Imaging-Dataset-Statistics-2016-05-19.pdf

13. Rachner, T.D., Khosla, S., Hofbauer, L.C.: Osteoporosis: now and the future. Lancet **377**(9773), 1276–1287 (2011)

14. Viola, P., Jones, M.: Rapid object detection using a boosted cascade of simple features. In: Proceeding of CVPR, pp. 511–518. IEEE Computer Society (2001)

15. Williams, A.L., Al-Busaidi, A., Sparrow, P.J., Adams, J.E., Whitehouse, R.W.: Under-reporting of osteoporotic vertebral fractures on computed tomography. Eur. J. Radiol. **69**(1), 179–183 (2009)

Global Localization and Orientation of the Cervical Spine in X-ray Images

S.M. Masudur Rahman Al Arif[1]([✉]), Michael Gundry[2], Karen Knapp[2], and Greg Slabaugh[1]

[1] Department of Computer Science, City, University of London, London, UK
S.Al-Arif@city.ac.uk
[2] University of Exeter Medical School, Exeter, UK

Abstract. Injuries in cervical spine X-ray images are often missed by emergency physicians. Many of these missing injuries cause further complications. Automated analysis of the images has the potential to reduce the chance of missing injuries. Towards this goal, this paper proposes an automatic localization of the spinal column in cervical spine X-ray images. The framework employs a random classification forest algorithm with a kernel density estimation-based voting accumulation method to localize the spinal column and to detect the orientation. The algorithm has been evaluated with 90 emergency room X-ray images and has achieved an average detection accuracy of 91% and an orientation error of 3.6°. The framework can be used to narrow the search area for other advanced injury detection systems.

Keywords: Random forest · Classification · Cervical · Vertebra · Localization · Orientation

1 Introduction

The cervical spine is vulnerable to high-impact accidents like automobile collision, sports mishaps and falls. Due to the scanning time required, cost, and the position of the spine in the human body, X-ray is the first mode of investigation for cervical spine injuries. Unfortunately, roughly 20% of cervical vertebrae related injuries remain undetected by emergency physicians and about 67% of these missing injuries result in tragic consequences like loss of motor control, disability to move the neck and other neurological deteriorations [1,2]. Providing emergency physicians with an automated analysis of the cervical X-ray images has a great potential to reduce the chances of missing injuries. Towards that goal, this paper takes the first step to localise the cervical spine in an arbitrary X-ray image. Our method involves a machine learning process which employs a patch based framework to localize the vertebrae column. It is also able to predict the orientation of the spinal curve.

© Springer International Publishing AG 2016
J. Yao et al. (Eds.): CSI 2016, LNCS 10182, pp. 64–76, 2016.
DOI: 10.1007/978-3-319-55050-3_6

Some limited work has been presented in the literature for global localization of the cervical spine on X-ray images. Most of the methods revolve around the generalized Hough transform (GHT). Tezmol et al. [3] used a GHT based framework using mean vertebra templates and an innovative voting accumulator structure. A more recent work [4], proposed another template matching based approach relying on GHT which involves a training phase. In contrast, our work is designed as a machine learning classification problem and votes are accumulated, then refined in a novel fashion to generate a bounding box.

Random forest is a popular machine learning algorithm [5]. It has been used in recent vertebra related literature [6–11]. Glocker et al. presented a random regression forest based localization and identification framework for vertebrae in arbitrary CT scans [10]. They proposed another framework using random classification forest which have shown better performance in localizing and identifying vertebrae with pathological cases [11]. Our work also uses random classification forest. But instead of localizing and identifying each vertebrae, it finds the global position and orientation of the vertebral column in cervical X-ray images.

The recent work by Bromiley et al. [6], demonstrated a segmentation method based on constrained local model (CLM) and random forest regression voting (RFRV). Like other statistical shape model (SSM)-based approaches [7,12], this work also requires initialization of the mean shape near the actual vertebra. The initialization is usually done with help of manual click points [6,12] or other automatic methods [7]. Random regression forest-based initialization method described in [7] requires a bounding box from where the input features are collected. In their work, the bounding box around the vertebrae curve is generated using hard parameters which are empirically found based on the training images. In our work, we propose an automatic way to locate the vertebrae column in X-ray images.

In this work, 90 cervical X-ray images of emergency room patients were evaluated. The images contain a total of 450 cervical vertebrae (C3–C7). A random forest is trained to distinguish between vertebra and non-vertebra image patches from the images. The task is designed as a binary classification problem: vertebra and non-vertebra. The framework employs a two-stage coarse-to-fine approach. In the first coarse localization stage, a sliding window sparsely scans a test image to vote for vertebrae patches. After this sparse voting, an accumulation phase converts the votes into a bounding box which indicates the position of the spinal column inside the image. The fine localization stage scans the resultant bounding box of the first stage densely with different patch sizes and orientations. The same voting accumulation phase is applied again and a refined bounding box is generated. The angle of this bounding box determines the predicted orientation of the vertebrae column. Even on a dataset of emergency room X-ray images, 91% of the vertebrae area has been detected under the first stage bounding box and an average error of 3.6° has been achieved for orientation prediction with the second stage bounding box.

2   Data

Our dataset of 90 lateral view emergency room X-ray images was collected from the Royal Devon and Exeter Hospital, and consists of patients exhibiting symptoms, ranging from pain to serious trauma. Different radiography systems were used. The resolution of the images were in the range from 0.1 to 0.194 mm per pixel and the exposure time varied from 16 to 345 ms. The ages of the patients were in the range from 18 to 91. All the scans were digital and taken in 2014–15. These images were anonymized and collected through appropriate procedures to be used for research.

Along with the data, our partners at University of Exeter have also provided manual segmentations of the vertebrae. A set of 20 landmark (LM) points per vertebra was annotated by experts in the field and these annotations were used in training and to evaluate the performance of our algorithm quantitatively. Figure 1a shows example images from our dataset and Fig. 1b shows manual segmentation points on a spine. For this work, vertebra C3 to C7 are considered. C1 and C2 are not studied as their appearance is ambiguous in lateral cervical X-ray images.

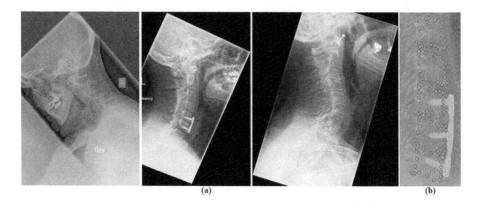

Fig. 1. (a) X-ray images in the dataset. (b) Manual segmentation points.

3   Methodology

The localization framework is based on the detection of vertebrae patches in the images. The detection is done by image patches where a machine learning algorithm decides whether the patch belongs to a vertebra or not. To learn this, a random classification forest [5] has been used. Image patches are generated from the image datasets and labelled into vertebra class and non-vertebra class. The patches are considered with different patch sizes and patch orientations. To generate positive patches, the manual segmentation of the vertebra points is used. The center of the vertebra is used as an anchor point on which different sizes and orientations are considered for training. In order to generate patches for the non-vertebra class, 50% of the patches are considered from both sides of the vertebral column and the rest are collected from other areas of the image. Figure 2a shows the areas from which the positive and negative patches are collected; positive patches are collected from the green box, 50% of the negatives patches are collected from the blue boxes and other negative patches are collected from the remainder of the image randomly. More importance is provided in the areas adjacent to the vertebral column for negative patch creation so that the forest has a better opportunity to distinguish these areas. These image patches are then converted to structured forest (SF) feature vectors [13,14]. This feature vector collects gradient magnitude and orientation information at different scales and angles. This feature vector recently has shown outstanding performance on the edge detection problem [14]. As vertebrae patches are mostly filled with edge-like structures, this feature vector is chosen. Once the feature vectors and corresponding binary output labels are ready, a random classification forest is trained on the data.

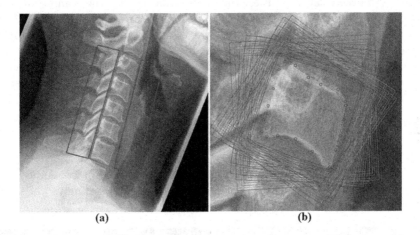

(a)   (b)

Fig. 2. (a) Area of positive patches (green box) and area of 50% of the negative patches (blue boxes). (b) Positive patch boundaries around a vertebra with different orientations and sizes. (Color figure online)

3.1 Stage 1: Coarse Localization

At test time, a new image is fed into the framework for localization. A set of test points is generated on the image at fixed step size (S_1). A single orientation $0°$ (O_1) and a fixed patch size, P_1, is considered to generate image patches, one at each of the test points. The generated image patches overlap neighbouring image patches. The amount of overlapping is controlled by the parameters S_1 and P_1. These patches are fed into the forest. The forest determines which test points belong to vertebrae. These positive predicted points, x_is, are then passed to the vote accumulation phase to generate a bounding box.

Vote Accumulator: The vote accumulator adds a Gaussian kernel at each of the positive votes. The bandwidth, t, of these kernels are automatically estimated using a diffusion-based technique proposed by Botev et al. [15]. This method allows the bandwidth (t) to change dynamically based on the vote distribution from image to image. The resultant distributions are then added together to form a single distribution, F, over the image space.

$$F(\boldsymbol{x}) = \frac{1}{N} \sum_{i=1}^{N} \frac{1}{\sqrt{2\pi t}} e^{-\frac{(\boldsymbol{x}-\boldsymbol{x}_i)^2}{2t}} \tag{1}$$

where N is the number of total positive votes coming to the accumulator.

This distribution over the image space is converted to a binary image, B, by dynamic thresholding (Eq. 2). The resulting binary image may be divided into a number of parts, B_js (Fig. 3c). The area of these parts are measured (A_j) and weighted (w_j) based on the distance from the image center (C_{image}) to the centroid of the concerned image part (C_{B_j}). As the images are taken to diagnose cervical vertebrae related injuries, the assumption is that the spine should be located near the image center, not at any extreme corner of the image. Then some of these areas are eliminated if they are small enough or located far from any adjacent areas (Eq. 6). This process reduces the chance of misdetection, for example, the area in the skull region of Fig. 3c. Finally, a minimal bounding parallelogram is generated to enclose the rest of areas [16]. This parallelogram is the output of the coarse localization stage. The process is summarized in Fig. 3.

$$B(\boldsymbol{x}) = \begin{cases} 1 & \text{if } F(\boldsymbol{x}) > F_t, \\ 0 & \text{otherwise.} \end{cases} \tag{2}$$

where $F_t = K \times max(F)$ and K is an empirically chosen constant. As $max(F)$ is different for different images, F_t dynamically changes accordingly.

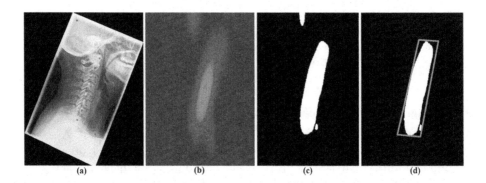

(a)   (b)   (c)   (d)

Fig. 3. (a) Positive votes on the image. (b) Resultant distribution F. (c) F after binarization. (d) F after elimination of invalid areas with the minimum bound parallelogram.

$$A_j = area(B_j) \tag{3}$$

$$w_j = \frac{1}{distance(C_{image}, C_{B_j})} \tag{4}$$

$$wA_j = A_j \times w_j \tag{5}$$

where $j = 1, 2, ..., M$; M is the number of disconnected areas in B and C_a denotes the centroid of the area a. In Fig. 3c $M = 3$.

$$\hat{B}_j = B_j = \begin{cases} valid \ (kept) & \text{if } wA_j > A_t \ \& \ d_{B_j} < d_t \\ invalid \ (eliminated) & \text{otherwise.} \end{cases} \tag{6}$$

$$d_{B_j} = minimum\Big(\big\{distance(C_{B_k}, C_{B_j}) : k\epsilon\{1, 2, ..., M\} \ and \ k \neq j\big\}\Big) \tag{7}$$

where A_t and d_j are the empirical area and distance threshold respectively.

$$BoundingBox_{coarse} = mBP\Big(\big\{\hat{B}_j : j\epsilon\{1, 2, ..., O\}\big\}\Big) \tag{8}$$

where mBP computes the minimum bound parallelogram enclosing the valid B_js [16] and O is the number of valid disconnected areas. In Fig. 3d $O = 2$.

3.2   Stage 2: Fine Localization

The previous stage is a single resolution single orientation phase, thus less probable to find vertebra with uncommon orientation or size. As the bounding box of the previous stage is only meant to find the approximate area covered by the vertebra, coarse localization is enough. But in order to find the orientation of the vertebrae curve, a finer localization with multiple patch resolutions and orientations is necessary. In this stage, a new set of test points is created within the coarse localization bounding box, with varying step sizes, S_2. At each test point, multiple patches are generated with different patch sizes (P_2) and angles (O_2). Then the same random forest patch classification and vote accumulation phase are conducted. This creates a refined bounding box within the first stage bounding box. The orientation angle of this smaller bounding box is computed as the orientation of the vertebrae column.

4   Experiment and Results

To train the random classification forest, different sizes and orientations of the image patches have been considered. The orientation of the patch is defined as the rotation of the angle from the mean vertebral axis. To train the forest, 7 different patch sizes with a step of 0.5 mm (starting from the vertebra size) and 19 orientations of $-45°$ to $+45°$ with a step of $5°$ have been used. From the 450 cervical vertebrae of our dataset, a total of $450 \times 7 \times 19 = 59,850$ vertebra (positive) images patches were generated. To balance the data, equal numbers of non-vertebra patches were generated from the rest part of each image. Each these image patches was converted to a SF feature vector of length 6116.

The random forest has a number free parameters: maximum allowable tree depth (nD), minimum number of sample at a node ($nMin$), number of trees ($nTree$) and number of variables to test at node split ($nVar$) and number of thresholds to choose from ($nThresh$). To find optimum parameters, a sequential parameter search has been applied to a fixed set of training and test images from the dataset. Final parameters are reported in Table 1. To measure the performance of the trained forest, a ten-fold cross-validation scheme is followed. For each fold, 10% of the images are considered as test images and others are used for forest training. Table 2 reports the patch classification accuracies of each forest.

The localization framework also has a set of free parameters mentioned in Sects. 3.1 and 3.2 which are empirically chosen and reported in Table 1. The localization algorithm has been applied on all the images and for each image, the forest was chosen from the ten forests such that the test image is not used in training. We have reported two metrics for the coarse localization bounding box: (1) Average percentage of vertebrae area covered inside the bounding box and (2) Average percentage of landmark points falling outside the bounding box. The orientation of the second stage bounding box is calculated based on the angle of the longer axis of the parallelogram with the horizontal axis. The ground truth orientation is measured by a smallest possible parallelogram that covers the

Table 1. Optimized parameters and values.

Parameters	Values
P_1	24 mm
S_1	10 mm
O_1	0
K	0.5
A_t	10 pixel
d_t	15 mm
P_2	20, 30, 40 mm
S_2	$P_2/2$
O_2	−45, 0, 45
nD	10
$nMin$	50
$nTree$	10
$nVar$	85
$nThresh$	5

Table 2. Patch classification accuracy of the forests.

Forest	Accuracy
Fold 1	97.90%
Fold 2	98.48%
Fold 3	95.34%
Fold 4	97.91%
Fold 5	98.21%
Fold 6	95.92%
Fold 7	97.63%
Fold 8	98.25%
Fold 9	97.62%
Fold 10	98.36%

Table 3. Performance of the coarse localization bounding box.

Vertebra	Percentage of area inside the bounding box			Percentage of landmark points outside the bounding box		
	Median	Mean	Std	Median	Mean	Std
C3	100%	97%	14%	0%	7%	16%
C4	100%	**99%**	4%	0%	**2%**	7%
C5	100%	97%	12%	0%	4%	14%
C6	100%	92%	22%	0%	11%	24%
C7	87%	69%	37%	33%	37%	36%
Overall	100%	91%	24%	0%	12%	25%

Table 4. Orientation error in degree(°): GTO: Ground truth orientation, ALMP: All landmark points, FLMP: Landmark points inside the first stage bounding box.

GTO type	Coarse localization		Fine localization	
	ALMP	FLMP	ALMP	FLMP
Median	5.73	3.89	3.07	2.37
Mean	8.16	6.26	4.59	**3.60**
Std	8.21	7.18	5.27	4.55

manual annotations (Fig. 4a). The error is calculated by the absolute different between the ground truth orientation and predicted orientation in degrees (°). The results are reported in Tables 3 and 4. Overall 91% of the vertebra area fell inside the predicted bounding box. Only 12% of the landmark points were outside the box. The best performance is achieved by the vertebra C4 at 99%, followed by C3 and C5 both at 97%. The performance is worse as we go down the spine, C6 reports 92% and C7 69%. In terms of percentage of landmark points falling outside the bounding box, from C3 to C7, the numbers are 7%, 2%, 4%, 11%, and 37%. Figure 5 demonstrates the metrics graphically. Almost 80% of the vertebrae have no parts of it outside the bounding box. In terms of landmark points, 70% the vertebrae have no LM points outside the bounding box and about 80% have less than three points out of 20 LM points (15%).

The orientation error metric can be computed in two ways. One with all the vertebrae (ALMP), C3–C7, the other with only the landmark points that fall inside the bounding box of the first stage (FLMP). As the second stage can only use the information what's inside the first stage bounding box, the later seems more fair to judge its ability. When considering all the vertebra the average error is 4.59° while the other results in an average of 3.6°. For the coarse localization bounding box the average errors are larger: 8.16° and 6.26° respectively.

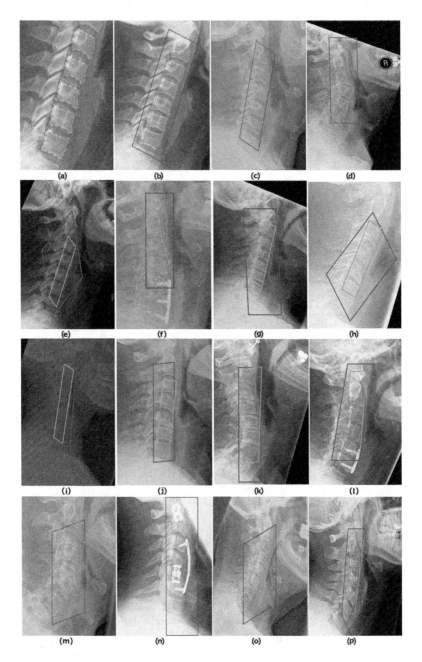

Fig. 4. (a) Manual annotation points and ground truth bounding box (green). (b)–(p) Coarse (blue) and fine (cyan) localization bounding boxes. (p) An example of the ongoing vertebral curve detection method (magenta). (Color figure online)

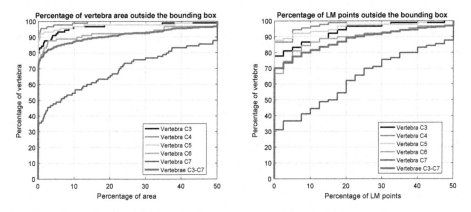

Fig. 5. Percentage of area and landmark points outside the coarse localization bounding box.

Table 5. Localization performance.

	Coarse localization			Fine localization		
	Dice coeff.	Sensitivity	Specificity	Dice coeff.	Sensitivity	Specificity
Median	0.65	0.93	0.97	0.71	0.61	1.00
Mean	0.62	0.88	0.97	0.69	0.62	0.99
Std	0.14	0.14	0.03	0.11	0.15	0.01

Table 5 reports the average Dice coefficient, sensitivity (true positive rate) and specificity (true negative rate) of the coarse and fine localization bounding boxes. These metrics are computed by comparing the ground truth bounding box (Fig. 4a) with predicted bounding boxes. The Dice coefficient for coarse localization bounding box averages at 0.62 where it stands at 0.69 for the fine localization bounding box. However in terms of sensitivity, the first stage bounding box scores 0.88 while the second stage bounding box scores only 0.62. Specificity is high for both bounding boxes: 0.97 for coarse localization and 0.99 for fine localization.

5   Discussion and Conclusion

In this work, a coarse to fine cervical spine localization algorithm has been evaluated on a set of 90 emergency room X-ray images. The algorithm is based on a random forest patch classifier which distinguishes between the vertebra and the non-vertebra image patches. Based on the centers of vertebra patches on a test image, a novel vote accumulator converts the votes into a bounding box. A second multi-resolution multi-orientation patch classification is applied inside the initial bounding box to determine the orientation of the vertebral column. The resultant coarse localization bounding box covers 91% of the all vertebral area on an average with a maximum of 99% for vertebra C4. C4's location on the spine is key to the increased accuracy. On average only 12% of the landmark points fell outside the bounding box, most of which are from the lowest vertebra, C7, where the image quality is often reduced.

While coarse localization creates a larger bounding box, the fine localization creates a smaller and refined bounding box. This bounding box predicts the orientation of the spinal column better. The average orientation error of the fine localization bounding box is 3.6° only while for the coarse bounding box, the error is 6.26°. The fine localization scans the coarse localization box with more variation and thus it can find the spinal orientation with better accuracy.

To measure the compactness of the both bounding boxes, Dice coefficients and sensitivity metrics are computed. The Dice coefficient of the fine localization bounding box is 9% higher than the Dice coefficient of the coarse localization box. However, in terms of sensitivity, coarse localization outperforms fine localization bounding box by 30%. Based on the application in which the bounding boxes will be used, the user may choose between the two options.

Our algorithms outperformed the performances of [3,4]. [3] reported an average orientation error of 4.16° and [4] reports a vertebra detection 89%. However, [3] report only 10% landmark points to be outside the bounding box which is lower than our 12%. But their landmark points did not consider the posterior points. It is also important to mention that both of these works, has been performed on a small (40 and 50) images from NHANES-II dataset of scanned X-ray images, where the images are collected from healthy patients for the purpose of developing automatic algorithms thus contains less variation, injuries and exposure differences. In our case, the dataset represents X-ray images collected from real life emergency room images where resolution, patient age, injury, orientation, X-ray exposure all vary widely. Figure 4 shows examples of images with low contrast (h, i), bone implants (f, l, n), displacements (j, m) and osteoporosis (d, k). Our algorithm works well in all these conditions.

The algorithm is written in MATLAB2014b on a Intel Core-i5 3 GHz machine with 8GB RAM and have not been optimized for execution time. The unoptimized code takes on average around 2.5 s to run the whole localization procedure (both coarse and fine). The execution time varies based on the image size, resolution and number of positive votes at each stage.

The performance of our algorithm can be attributed to the training of the forests and to the novel voting accumulation process. The patch classification accuracy of forests is in the range of 95 to 98% (Table 2) which eliminates the majority of the false detections. The novel voting accumulation method which utilises dynamic diffusion based kernel density estimation and weighted area filtering eliminates the rest of the false detection and thus the final results are good. We are currently working on a vertebral curve detection method (Fig. 4(p)), which can detect the anterior and posterior vertebral curves. A single orientation angle is not capable of describing the spinal column accurately. In many cases, the spinal column is a curve than a straight line (Fig. 4(d, m)). Thus, these curves will tell us more about the global orientation of the spine. Our next target is to detect the vertebrae centers or other landmarks automatically like [6–9]. The output of this work will be helpful in order to limit our search over the image. It can also help algorithms [7–9] where the search area was manually reduced with hard coded parameters.

References

1. Platzer, P., Hauswirth, N., Jaindl, M., Chatwani, S., Vecsei, V., Gaebler, C.: Delayed or missed diagnosis of cervical spine injuries. J. Trauma Acute Care Surg. **61**(1), 150–155 (2006)
2. Morris, C., McCoy, E.: Clearing the cervical spine in unconscious polytrauma victims, balancing risks and effective screening. Anaesthesia **59**(5), 464–482 (2004)
3. Tezmol, A., Sari-Sarraf, H., Mitra, S., Long, R., Gururajan, A.: Customized hough transform for robust segmentation of cervical vertebrae from x-ray images. In: Fifth IEEE Southwest Symposium on Image Analysis and Interpretation, Proceedings, pp. 224–228. IEEE (2002)
4. Larhmam, M.A., Mahmoudi, S., Benjelloun, M.: Semi-automatic detection of cervical vertebrae in X-ray images using generalized hough transform. In: 2012 3rd International Conference on Image Processing Theory, Tools and Applications (IPTA), pp. 396–401. IEEE (2012)
5. Breiman, L.: Random forests. Mach. Learn. **45**(1), 5–32 (2001)
6. Bromiley, P.A., Adams, J.E., Cootes, T.: Localisation of vertebrae on DXA images using constrained local models with random forest regression voting. In: Yao, J., Glocker, B., Kinder, T., Li, S. (eds.) Recent Advances in Computational Methods and Clinical Applications for Spine Imaging. LNCVB, pp. 159–171. Springer, Heidelberg (2015)
7. Roberts, M.G., Cootes, T.F., Adams, J.E.: Automatic location of vertebrae on DXA images using random forest regression. In: Ayache, N., Delingette, H., Golland, P., Mori, K. (eds.) MICCAI 2012. LNCS, vol. 7512, pp. 361–368. Springer, Heidelberg (2012). doi:10.1007/978-3-642-33454-2_45
8. Al-Arif, S.M.M.R., Asad, M., Knapp, K., Gundry, M., Slabaugh, G.: Hough forest-based corner detection for cervical spine radiographs. In: Proceedings of the 19th Conference on Medical Image Understanding and Analysis (MIUA), pp. 183–188 (2015)
9. Al-Arif, S.M.M.R., Asad, M., Knapp, K., Gundry, M., Slabaugh, G.: Cervical vertebral corner detection using Haar-like features and modified Hough forest. In: 2015 5th International Conference on Image Processing Theory, Tools and Applications (IPTA). IEEE (2015)
10. Glocker, B., Feulner, J., Criminisi, A., Haynor, D.R., Konukoglu, E.: Automatic localization and identification of vertebrae in arbitrary field-of-view CT scans. In: Ayache, N., Delingette, H., Golland, P., Mori, K. (eds.) MICCAI 2012. LNCS, vol. 7512, pp. 590–598. Springer, Heidelberg (2012). doi:10.1007/978-3-642-33454-2_73
11. Glocker, B., Zikic, D., Konukoglu, E., Haynor, D.R., Criminisi, A.: Vertebrae localization in pathological spine CT via dense classification from sparse annotations. In: Mori, K., Sakuma, I., Sato, Y., Barillot, C., Navab, N. (eds.) MICCAI 2013. LNCS, vol. 8150, pp. 262–270. Springer, Heidelberg (2013). doi:10.1007/978-3-642-40763-5_33
12. Benjelloun, M., Mahmoudi, S., Lecron, F.: A framework of vertebra segmentation using the active shape model-based approach. J. Biomed. Imaging **2011**, 9 (2011)

13. Dollár, P., Zitnick, C.L.: Structured forests for fast edge detection. In: ICCV (2013)
14. Dollár, P., Zitnick, C.L.: Fast edge detection using structured forests. In: PAMI (2015)
15. Botev, Z.I., Grotowski, J.F., Kroese, D.P., et al.: Kernel density estimation via diffusion. Ann. Stat. **38**(5), 2916–2957 (2010)
16. Schwarz, C., Teich, J., Welzl, E., Evans, B.: On finding a minimal enclosing parallelogram. Citeseer (1994)

Accurate Intervertebral Disc Localisation and Segmentation in MRI Using Vantage Point Hough Forests and Multi-atlas Fusion

Mattias P. Heinrich[1(✉)] and Ozan Oktay[2]

[1] Institute of Medical Informatics, University of Lübeck, Lübeck, Germany
heinrich@imi.uni-luebeck.de
[2] Biomedical Image Analysis Group, Imperial College London, London, UK
http://www.mpheinrich.de

Abstract. An accurate method for localising and segmenting interverte-bral discs in magnetic resonance (MR) spine imaging is presented. Atlas-based labelling of discs in MRI is challenging due to the small field of view and repetitive structures, which may cause the image registration to converge to a local minimum. To tackle this initialisation problem, our approach uses **Vantage Point Hough Forests** to automatically and robustly regress landmark positions, which are used to initialise a dis-crete deformable registration of all training images. An image-adaptive fusion of propagated segmentation labels is obtained by non-negative least-squares regression. Despite its simplicity and without using specific domain knowledge, our approach achieves sub-voxel localisation accuracy of 0.61 mm, Dice segmentation overlaps of nearly 90% (for the training data) and takes less than ten minutes to process a new scan.

1 Introduction and Related Work

Automatic analysis of vertebras intervertabral discs in clinical 3D volumes of the spine is useful for diagnosis, monitoring of disease progression, image-guided surgical interventions and population studies [16]. While segmenting and local-ising vertebra bodies have been predominantly performed in CT scans [8,9,15], the soft tissue contrast and non-ionising acquisition of magnetic resonance imag-ing (MRI) makes it the preferred modality for intervertabral disc analysis [2,3]. Automated analysis of spine images, which has seen increased research interest over the last years (also due to the *SpineWeb*[1] initiative), is challenging due to the repetitive appearance of vertebras, restricted field-of-views. Therefore apply-ing standard segmentation propagation approaches (multi-atlas segmentation) can easily fail [9] and/or require very long processing times. Thus model-based approaches [15], the integration of graphical model information [4,19] as well as regression forests [2,3,8] have been employed to increase robustness for finding and labelling the correct structures. The goal of the *"Automatic Intervertebral Disc Localization and Segmentation from 3D Multi-modality MR (M3) Images"*

---

[1] http://spineweb.digitalimaginggroup.ca.

© Springer International Publishing AG 2016
J. Yao et al. (Eds.): CSI 2016, LNCS 10182, pp. 77–84, 2016.
DOI: 10.1007/978-3-319-55050-3_7

challenge held in conjunction with MICCAI 2016 is the identification, localisation and segmentation of seven discs, which are mainly within the lumbar spine.

Our work follows a similar methodological approach as [2,9]. First, we robustly localise the 3D position of the seven discs using a combination of a regression forest, Hough accumulation and a graphical model. Second, we use these positions to initialise a fast, discrete multi-atlas registration framework, which is followed by a non-negative least-squares regression of the most likely segmentation label. These 3D segmentations are then employed to refine the localisation estimation. While we build upon previous work, our approach contains elements that are (to the best of our knowledge) new to automatic spine segmentation/localisation. First, instead of using a supervised axis-parallel regression forest we adapt the recent concept of vantage-point forests [12] for regression, which has been shown to outperform random forests for multi-organ segmentation. Here, the whole length of a binary context feature vector is used to cluster the data meaningfully without being reliant on ground truth information during tree generation. Second, the combination of very fast deformable registration [10] and regression-based label fusion algorithms [14] enables processing times of less than ten minutes for a multi-atlas label fusion (MALF) reducing the time requirements compared to most state-of-the-art approaches substantially.

The paper is outlined as follows: we begin by describing our vantage point regression forests in Sect. 2, which is followed by a vote accumulation in Hough space and a simple spatial regularisation of candidates using a graphical (Markov chain) model for an accurate prediction of all disc centres in a new unseen scan. Note, that our approach does not make any specific use of domain knowledge and would therefore be applicable to other anatomical localisation tasks. Afterwards, the multi-atlas registration and label fusion framework is presented based on [10,14] in Sect. 3. A detailed flow-chart of all algorithmic steps is presented in Fig. 1. Finally, we present our experiments and results on the training dataset of the challenge in Sect. 4 and discuss our conclusion in Sect. 5. Note, that currently

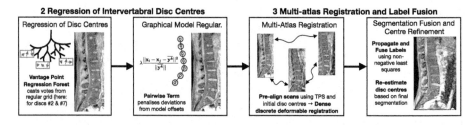

Fig. 1. Flow-chart of our proposed algorithm for accurate intervertebral disc localisation and segmentation. First, initial locations of disc centres are robustly found using vantage point forests and a graphical model. Next, the disc centres are used as known correspondences to initialise a deformable registration using a thin-plate spline (TPS) warp. Finally, multi-atlas label fusion is performed for accurate voxelwise segmentation and a refinement of disc centres.

we only employ the standard proton MRI sequence, but further improvements are to be expected when using all multi-modal scans.

2   Regression of Intervertabral Disc Centres

In order to analyse new scans completely automatically a robust initialisation of the correct disc positions is often necessary. A common problem for disc localisation in MR spine images is the confusion of two neighbouring discs due to their similarity and missing anatomical context (abdominal organs are not clearly visible in the field-of-view). We build our regression upon the recent concept of vantage point forests [12]. Since, a global localisation is sought, we sample patches on a uniform grid of locations $\mathbf{x}_i$ across the whole image domain. In training the position of seven ground-truth disc centres $\mathbf{y}_k$ is obtained as the centre of mass of the provided segmentation masks.

An intensity patch $\mathcal{P}_i \in \mathbb{R}^{|L|}$ (with L being the set of voxels), which is smoothed by a Gaussian kernel with variance σ_p^2, will be represented by a feature vector $\mathbf{h}_i \in \mathbb{H}^n$, where $h_{id} \in \{\pm 1\}$ defines the d-th dimension of the vector h_{id} corresponding to sample i. For this specific application, we restrict the feature values to be binary (in Hamming space $\mathbb{H}^n$) and can be simply obtained by a comparison of two random locations (q, r) within the patch:

$$h_{id} = +1 \text{ if } \mathcal{P}_i(q) > \mathcal{P}_i(r) \quad \text{for } (q, r) \in L \text{ and } h_{id} = -1 \text{ else} \qquad (1)$$

as done in previous work on organ or keypoint localisation [1,17]. Note, that the same random sampling layout is used for every location. The use of binary features improves robustness against contrast variations often present in MRI scans [17]. The vantage point tree [20] is a data-structure that is suitable to cluster high-dimensional feature spaces into nested hyperspheres. In contrast to previous work on regression forests for landmark localisation [4,8], we **do not** perform supervised node optimisation but simply choose a random data point j from the current node (vantage point) for clustering as follows. The Hamming distance $d_H(i, j) = \|\mathbf{h}_i - \mathbf{h}_j\|_{\mathbb{H}}$ (of the whole feature vectors) to all other data points i within the current node is calculated and the median distance τ is used as threshold to split the data into two equal-sized sets that form the left and right predecessor (child) nodes (see [12] for more details and an implementation). When reaching the leaf node a displacement vector $\mathbf{d}_i^k = \mathbf{y}^k - \mathbf{x}_i$ is stored for every sample i and every landmark $k \in \{1, 2, \ldots, 7\}$. Using the full binary feature vectors enables very discriminative splits even without explicitly modelling the distribution of displacement vectors and is computationally very efficient due to the implementation of the Hamming weight as popcount instruction in current CPUs [1]. A distance threshold $\delta_{\max}$ can be used to discard votes (during testing) from very far away locations. An ensemble of several randomly different vantage point trees is built to increase the generalisation.

During test the same random sampling layout is used as in Eq. 1 to extract binary feature vectors for a set of regular grid locations $\mathbf{x}_i$. After traversing each tree all training exemplars are collected and only the displacement vote of the one $(\mathbf{d}_{i*})$ with lowest Hamming distance with respect to the test sample is retained. Effectively, vantage point forests enable a very efficient approximate nearest neighbour search in Hamming space. The votes of all test locations (with offset vectors $\mathbf{x}_i + \mathbf{d}_{i*}^k$) are accumulated in 7 Hough volumes $\mathbf{H}^k$ (one for each landmark, cf. [4,6]), which are later smoothed by a Parzen window kernel with σ_H. Finally, a graphical model [18] is used to impose spatial constraints and avoid confusions of neighbouring discs (which occurred twice for all 56 discs in training). Dynamic programming is applied to all possible pair-wise combinations of candidates of neighbouring discs. The unary term for the model is chosen to be the negative exponential of the accumulated Hough votes for any image location, which results in probability maps $\mathbf{H}^k$ of same size as the input image. The pairwise regularisation cost (weighted by λ) is the squared Euclidean distance between (average) model offset $\overline{\mathbf{y}^k} = \frac{1}{n}\sum_{i=1}^{n}(\mathbf{y}_i^k - \mathbf{y}_i^{k+1})$ and difference between the two respective locations:

$$E(\mathbf{x}_i, \mathbf{x}_j, k, \mathbf{H}) = \exp(-\mathbf{H}^k(\mathbf{x}_i)) + \lambda\frac{||\mathbf{x}_i - \mathbf{x}_j - \overline{\mathbf{y}^k}||^2}{||\overline{\mathbf{y}^k}||} \tag{2}$$

The minimum of $E(\mathbf{x}_i, \mathbf{x}_j, k, \mathbf{H})$ for each possible combination $(\mathbf{x}_i, \mathbf{x}_j)$ for two connected landmarks $(k, k+1)$ can be computed in linear complexity using distance transforms of sampled functions [5]. Marginal distributions of the likelihood (or vice-versa uncertainty) of the position of all landmark positions can be obtained following [11,19].

3   Multi-atlas Registration and Label Fusion

The publicly available non-parametric discrete registration tool **deeds** of [10] was used due to its computational efficiency and good results for MRI segmentation propagation. Given the estimated landmark localisations for a test scan (using the outcome of the previous section) and the ground truth information in training scans, we generate bounding boxes (using average disc sizes) and match a thin-plate spline transformation to their corner points. This transformation is used to pre-align all training images (and segmentation masks). Local cross correlation with a radius of $r = 3$ was used as similarity metric together with a Gaussian smoothing of 1.2 voxels and symmetry constraint for regularisation. The default multi-resolution and search range settings were used. Each deformable registration took around 60 s.

Following the well-known concept of multi-atlas label fusion (MALF), we estimate a local weighting for each (of the 7) registered atlas scan based on local cross correlation and a non-negative least square regression [14]. This step produces spatially coherent and accurate disc segmentations (see Fig. 2(c)), is very fast in practise ($\approx$10 s), and can effectively compensate registration errors. Afterwards, the disc locations are re-estimated as the centre of mass of the fused segmentation labels for improved accuracy.

4   Experiments and Results on Training Data

In our experiments the combination of vantage point forests, Hough aggregation and this simple graphical model (see example results in Fig. 2) achieved very robust results (without a single misclassification of intervertebral discs) and required less tuning than random regression forests (for which we could not find sufficient settings for all training cases). We smoothed patches with $\sigma_p = 2.5$ mm, used $n = 320$ binary features drawn randomly within a radius of 25 mm, a stride of 4 voxels for the regular grid of voting voxels $\mathbf{x}_i$, and built 15 trees with a leaf size termination of 5. The application of the model to a test scan took approx. 2 s (including Hough aggregation and graphical model). The Parzen kernel for Hough aggregation was $\sigma_H = 3.75$ mm, the distance threshold $\delta_{max} = 37.5$ mm and the regularisation weighting $\lambda = 2$. We obtained an average localisation error of 7.09 mm (max: 39 mm) without and 3.87 mm (max: 10 mm) with graphical model (see Table 1). While a lower error could easily be achieved by including a (cascaded) refinement stage [3,7], we are here mainly interested in the robustness of this step, since small misalignments will easily be corrected by the following deformable registration. After applying the multi-atlas registration and label fusion of Sect. 3, we achieve very high segmentation overlap (with an average Dice of 0.89) and a very low disc location error of 0.69 mm (the scan resolution is 1.25 mm^3) using the centre-of-mass re-estimation.

Table 1. Quantitative evaluation of our vantage point Hough forest regression (VPF). The robustness is increased by a subsequent graphical model (MRF). When used to initialise a fast multi-atlas registration and label fusion (MALF), very low localisation and segmentation surface distances as well as high Dice scores are achieved.

Method	Metric	avg.	#1	#2	#3	#4	#5	#6	#7	#8
MALF w/o regr.	Localisation (mm)	**5.51**	0.75	37.58	2.79	0.48	0.71	0.53	0.79	0.50
	Surface dist. (mm)	**3.34**	0.52	19.92	3.65	0.56	0.44	0.39	0.40	0.85
	Dice overlap	**0.76**	0.89	0.02	0.70	0.90	0.88	0.89	0.90	0.88
VPF+Hough	Localisation (mm)	**7.09**	4.10	12.44	12.60	9.25	3.44	2.52	5.58	6.80
	Loc. max (mm)		5.72	39.89	38.41	39.81	5.32	5.79	26.82	27.31
+MRF	Localisation (mm)	**3.87**	3.87	2.90	3.78	5.25	3.08	4.16	3.91	3.97
	Loc. max (mm)		5.51	7.07	6.38	8.93	5.50	7.86	7.68	10.05
+MALF	Localisation (mm)	**0.61**	0.76	0.57	0.52	0.53	0.68	0.50	0.84	0.50
	Surface dist. (mm)	**0.38**	0.37	0.39	0.39	0.38	0.36	0.36	0.35	0.39
	Dice overlap	**0.89**	0.89	0.89	0.90	0.91	0.89	0.89	0.90	0.88

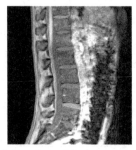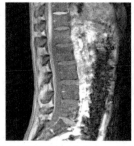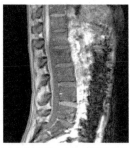

(a) Overlay with ground truth (b) MALF with linear init. (c) MALF with VPF init.

Fig. 2. Sagittal slice of 3D MRI of *case B* with segmentations of all seven discs overlaid in colour. (a) Ground truth manual segmentation. (b) Misaligned segmentations using standard multi-atlas label fusion (MALF) due to poor initialisation. (c) Proposed vantage point forest regression improves overlap and successfully segments all discs as it provides better initialisation for MALF. Best viewed in colour. (Color figure online)

5   Discussion

We have presented a simple yet very robust and fast method for finding anatomical landmarks (intervertebral discs) in spine MRI scans. The use of (unsupervised) vantage point forest together with discriminative binary feature vectors enables very good regression results without tuning of different trade-offs between classification and regression in supervised random forests. A subsequent multi-atlas registration and label fusion (initialised using a thin-plate spline transform obtained from this automatic disc localisation) achieve a Dice score of 89% on average and a refined average localisation error of 0.69 mm with a processing time of ≈10 min per unseen scan. Further improvements may be obtained by employing all multi-channel MR sequences (here we only used the proton MRI), which could be easily integrated using [13]. The source-code for all processing steps will be made available on http://mpheinrich.de/software.html.

References

1. Calonder, M., Lepetit, V., Ozuysal, M., Trzcinski, T., Strecha, C., Fua, P.: BRIEF: computing a local binary descriptor very fast. IEEE PAMI **34**(7), 1281–1298 (2012)
2. Chen, C., Belavy, D., Yu, W., Chu, C., Armbrecht, G., Bansmann, M., Felsenberg, D., Zheng, G.: Localization and segmentation of 3D intervertebral discs in MR images by data driven estimation. IEEE Trans. Med. Imag. **34**(8), 1719–1729 (2015)
3. Chen, C., Belavy, D., Zheng, G.: 3D intervertebral disc localization and segmentation from MR images by data-driven regression and classification. In: Wu, G., Zhang, D., Zhou, L. (eds.) MLMI 2014. LNCS, vol. 8679, pp. 50–58. Springer, Cham (2014). doi:10.1007/978-3-319-10581-9_7
4. Donner, R., Menze, B.H., Bischof, H., Langs, G.: Global localization of 3D anatomical structures by pre-filtered hough forests and discrete optimization. Med. Image Anal. **17**(8), 1304–1314 (2013)

5. Felzenszwalb, P.F., Huttenlocher, D.P.: Distance transforms of sampled functions. Theory Comput. **8**, 415–428 (2012)
6. Gall, J., Yao, A., Razavi, N., Van Gool, L., Lempitsky, V.: Hough forests for object detection, tracking, and action recognition. IEEE Trans. Pattern Anal. Mach. Intell. **33**(11), 2188–2202 (2011)
7. Gauriau, R., Cuingnet, R., Lesage, D., Bloch, I.: Multi-organ localization with cascaded global-to-local regression and shape prior. Med. Image Anal. **23**(1), 70–83 (2015)
8. Glocker, B., Feulner, J., Criminisi, A., Haynor, D.R., Konukoglu, E.: Automatic localization and identification of vertebrae in arbitrary field-of-view CT scans. In: Ayache, N., Delingette, H., Golland, P., Mori, K. (eds.) MICCAI 2012. LNCS, vol. 7512, pp. 590–598. Springer, Heidelberg (2012). doi:10.1007/978-3-642-33454-2_73
9. Glocker, B., Zikic, D., Haynor, D.R.: Robust registration of longitudinal spine CT. In: Golland, P., Hata, N., Barillot, C., Hornegger, J., Howe, R. (eds.) MICCAI 2014. LNCS, vol. 8673, pp. 251–258. Springer, Cham (2014). doi:10.1007/978-3-319-10404-1_32
10. Heinrich, M.P., Papież, B.W., Schnabel, J.A., Handels, H.: Non-parametric discrete registration with convex optimisation. In: Ourselin, S., Modat, M. (eds.) WBIR 2014. LNCS, vol. 8545, pp. 51–61. Springer, Cham (2014). doi:10.1007/978-3-319-08554-8_6
11. Heinrich, M.P., Simpson, I.J., Papież, B.W., Brady, M., Schnabel, J.A.: Deformable image registration by combining uncertainty estimates from supervoxel belief propagation. Med. Image Anal. **27**, 57–71 (2016)
12. Heinrich, M.P., Blendowski, M.: Multi-organ segmentation using vantage point forests and binary context features. In: Ourselin, S., Joskowicz, L., Sabuncu, M.R., Unal, G., Wells, W. (eds.) MICCAI 2016. LNCS, vol. 9901, pp. 598–606. Springer, Cham (2016). doi:10.1007/978-3-319-46723-8_69
13. Heinrich, M.P., Papież, B.W., Schnabel, J.A., Handels, H.: Multispectral image registration based on local canonical correlation analysis. In: Golland, P., Hata, N., Barillot, C., Hornegger, J., Howe, R. (eds.) MICCAI 2014. LNCS, vol. 8673, pp. 202–209. Springer, Cham (2014). doi:10.1007/978-3-319-10404-1_26
14. Heinrich, M.P., Wilms, M., Handels, H.: Multi-atlas segmentation using patch-based joint label fusion with non-negative least squares regression. In: Wu, G., Coupé, P., Zhan, Y., Munsell, B., Rueckert, D. (eds.) Patch-MI 2015. LNCS, vol. 9467, pp. 146–153. Springer, Cham (2015). doi:10.1007/978-3-319-28194-0_18
15. Klinder, T., Ostermann, J., Ehm, M., Franz, A., Kneser, R., Lorenz, C.: Automated model-based vertebra detection, identification, and segmentation in CT images. Med. Image Anal. **13**(3), 471–482 (2009)
16. Li, S., Yao, J., Navab, N.: Guest editorial special issue on spine imaging, image-based modeling, and image guided intervention. IEEE Trans. Med. Imag. **34**(8), 1625–1626 (2015)
17. Pauly, O., Glocker, B., Criminisi, A., Mateus, D., Möller, A.M., Nekolla, S., Navab, N.: Fast multiple organ detection and localization in whole-body MR dixon sequences. In: Fichtinger, G., Martel, A., Peters, T. (eds.) MICCAI 2011. LNCS, vol. 6893, pp. 239–247. Springer, Heidelberg (2011). doi:10.1007/978-3-642-23626-6_30
18. Potesil, V., Kadir, T., Platsch, G., Brady, M.: Improved anatomical landmark localization in medical images using dense matching of graphical models. In: BMVC, vol. 4, p. 9 (2010)

19. Richmond, D., Kainmueller, D., Glocker, B., Rother, C., Myers, G.: Uncertainty-driven forest predictors for vertebra localization and segmentation. In: Navab, N., Hornegger, J., Wells, W.M., Frangi, A.F. (eds.) MICCAI 2015. LNCS, vol. 9349, pp. 653–660. Springer, Cham (2015). doi:10.1007/978-3-319-24553-9_80
20. Yianilos, P.N.: Data structures and algorithms for nearest neighbor search in general metric spaces. In: SODA 1993, pp. 311–321 (1993)

Multi-scale and Modality Dropout Learning for Intervertebral Disc Localization and Segmentation

Xiaomeng Li[✉], Qi Dou, Hao Chen, Chi-Wing Fu, and Pheng-Ann Heng

Department of Computer Science and Engineering,
The Chinese University of Hong Kong, Hong Kong, China
xmli@cse.cuhk.edu.hk

Abstract. Automatic localization and segmentation of intervertebral discs (IVDs) from volumetric magnetic resonance (MR) images is important for spine disease diagnosis. It dramatically alleviates the workload of radiologists given that the traditional manual annotation is time-consuming and error-prone with limited reproducibility. Compared with single modality data, multi-modality MR images are able to provide complementary information. However, how to effectively integrate them to generate more accurate segmentation results still remains open for studies. In this paper, we introduce a multi-scale and modality dropout learning framework to segment IVDs from four-modality MR images. Specifically, we design a 3D fully convolutional network which takes multiple scales of images as input and merges these pathways at higher layers to jointly integrate multi-scale information. Furthermore, in order to harness the complementary information from different modalities, we propose a modality dropout strategy to alleviate the co-adaption issue during the training. We evaluated our method on the *MICCAI 2016 Challenge on Automatic Intervertebral Disc Localization and Segmentation from 3D Multi-modality MR Images*. Our method achieved the best overall performance with the mean segmentation Dice as 91.2% and localization error as 0.62 mm, which demonstrated the superiority of our proposed framework.

1 Introduction

Accurate localization and segmentation of intervertebral discs (IVDs) from volumetric magnetic resonance (MR) images plays an important role for spine disease related diagnosis. Automatic localization and segmentation of IVDs are quite challenging due to the large intra-class variations and similar appearance among different IVDs.

Previous methods segmented the IVDs by employing hand-crafted features which were derived based on intensity and shape information [2,8,12]. However, these hand-crafted features tend to suffer from limited representation capability compared with the automatically learned features. Furthermore, these methods were usually performed based on 2D slices which might neglect the volumetric

J. Yao et al. (Eds.): CSI 2016, LNCS 10182, pp. 85–91, 2016.
DOI: 10.1007/978-3-319-55050-3_8

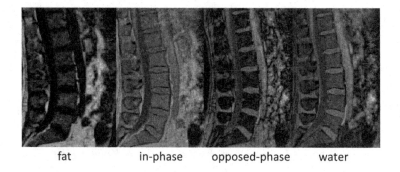

fat   in-phase   opposed-phase   water

Fig. 1. Illustration of IVD appearance in multi-modality MR images.

spatial contexts, thus degrading the performance. Recently, deep learning based methods have been proposed to directly localize and segment IVDs or vertebrae from volumetric data [4,7,10,14]. For example, Jamaludin *et al.* [10] proposed a convolutional neural network (CNN) framework to automatically label each disc and the surrounding vertebrae with a number of radiological scores. Chen *et al.* [5] introduced a 3D fully convolutional network (FCN) to localize and segment IVDs, which has achieved the state-of-the-art localization performance in MICCAI 2015 IVD localization and segmentation challenge.

Those previous works employed single modality MR data instead of taking multi-modality information into consideration, which would limit the localization and segmentation accuracy. Multi-modality MR images (see Fig. 1) collected by setting different scanning configurations can provide comprehensive information for robust diagnosis and treatment. Previous studies on brain segmentation indicated that multi-modality data could help to improve the segmentation performance significantly [3,6,15]. Meanwhile, incorporating multi-scale information into the learning process can further improve the performance [6,11].

In these regards, we propose a 3D multi-scale and modality dropout learning framework for localizing and segmenting IVDs from multi-modality MR images. Our contribution in this paper is twofold. First, we propose a novel multi-scale 3D fully convolutional network which consists of three pathways to integrate multiple scales of spatial information. Second, we propose a modality drop strategy for harnessing the complementary information from multi-modality MR data. Experimental results on the *MICCAI 2016 Challenge on Automatic Intervertebral Disc Localization and Segmentation from 3D Multi-modality MR Images* have demonstrated the superiority of our proposed framework.

2   Method

Figure 2 presents an overview of our proposed multi-scale and modality dropout learning framework based on multi-modality MR images. Our multi-scale fully convolutional network consists of three pathways with each inputting a different scale of volumetric image. In each training iteration, modality dropout strategy is

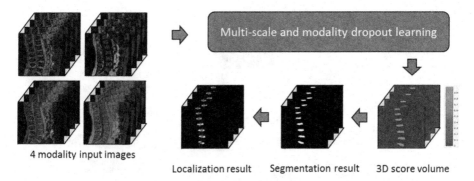

Fig. 2. An overview of our proposed multi-scale and modality dropout learning framework for IVDs segmentation and localization from multi-modality MR images

used on the input multi-modality data in order to reduce the feature co-adaption and encourage each single modality image to provide discriminative information.

2.1 Multi-scale FCN Architecture

One limitation of previous methods for IVDs segmentation is that they usually considered a single scale of spatial information surrounding the discs. However, multi-scale contextual information can contribute to better recognition performance. With this consideration, we employ multi-scale fully convolutional neural network with different scales of input data volumes. Figure 3 shows details of our proposed architecture, indicating input patch sizes, construction of layers, and kernel size and numbers. This multi-scale architecture consists of three pathways corresponding to different input volume sizes. During the training phase, three selected modality volumes (with one modality being randomly dropped) are input to the architecture. A 3D probability map with voxelwise predictions is generated as the output of the network. The final segmentation results can be determined from the score volume while the localization results can be generated as the centroids of the segmentation masks. In the experiments, we observe that the number of IVD voxels is much less than background voxels. To deal with the problem of imbalanced training samples, we employed weighted loss function during the training process, as shown in the following:

$$\mathcal{L} = \frac{1}{N} \sum_{i=1}^{N} [-w \cdot t_i \log p(x_i) - (1 - t_i) \log(1 - p(x_i))] \tag{1}$$

where w is the weight for strengthening the importance of foreground voxels. N denotes the total number of voxels in each training process, t_i denotes the label at voxel i and $p(x_i)$ denotes the corresponding prediction for voxel x_i.

2.2 Dropout Modality Learning

Dropout technique was proposed in [9,13] and it has been recognized as an effective way to prevent co-adaption of feature detectors and alleviate the overfitting

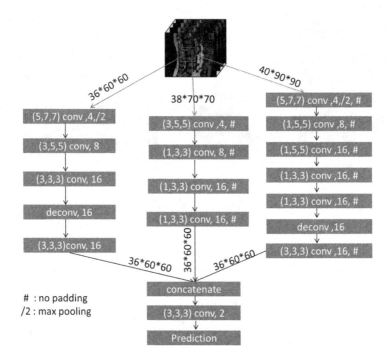

Fig. 3. The architecture of our proposed 3D multi-scale FCN. The red, blue and green boxes represent different scales of input to three different pathways. We only include one modality in this figure for clear illustration of the multi-scale framework. In experiments, the inputs are actually multi-modality images. (Color figure online)

problem. In our task of IVD localization and segmentation from multi-modality MR images, an intuitive approach is to input all modality data into the network for training. However, training four modality volumes all together may cause too much dependency among modalities, which leads to feature co-adaption and thus degrades the performance. Therefore, in order to fully take advantage of the complementary information from different modalities, we randomly dropped one modality during each training iteration to break the co-adaption and encourage harnessing discriminative information from remaining modalities. This can be regarded as a regularization on the optimization of neural networks. In the testing phase, we took all the four modality images as the input and generated the final segmentation and localization results.

3   Experiment

3.1   Dataset and Preprocessing

We evaluated our method on the dataset from *2016 MICCAI Challenge on Automatic Intervertebral Disc Localization and Segmentation from 3D Multi-modality*

MR Images [1]. The dataset was collected from a study investigating the effects of prolonged bed rest on lumbar intervertebral discs. The training data contains volumetric images from 8 patients and each subject consists of four modality MR datasets, i.e., in-phase, opposed-phase, fat and water. There are at least 7 IVDs in each image (size $36 \times 256 \times 256$). These multi-modality images of each subject are well registered and one binary mask is provided by manual annotation from radiologists. The testing data includes 6 subjects with ground truth held out by the organizers for independent evaluation.

3.2   On-site Competition Results

The evaluation metric for IVDs localization is mean localization distance (MLD) with standard deviation (SD), where MLD measures the accuracy of localization and SD quantifies the degree of variation. For IVDs segmentation evaluation, Mean Dice Overlap Coefficients (MDOC) and standard deviation (SDDOC) are used to measure the accuracy and variation of segmentation results. Mean Average Absolute Distance (MASD) with standard deviation (SDASD) is another measurement for evaluating segmentation accuracy. More details can be found on the challenge website [1]. Table 1 and Fig. 4 show the on-site challenge results. Our method achieved the performance of MDOC as 91.2% and MLD as 0.62 mm, which demonstrated the superiority of our proposed framework. We achieved the first place out of 3 teams during the on-site challenge according to the overall performance of these measurements.

Table 1. IVDs localization and segmentation results of our method in on-site challenge.

	MLD (mm)	SD	MDOC (%)	SDDOC	MASD (mm)	SDASD	Rank
Ours	0.62	0.38	91.2	1.8	1.26	1.22	1

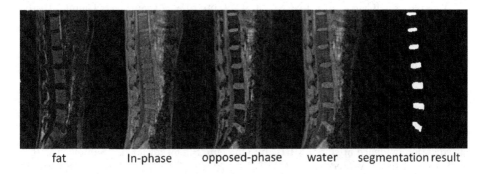

| fat | In-phase | opposed-phase | water | segmentation result |

Fig. 4. Example of on-site challenge results from one testing patient. We show one slice of the 3D volumetric data for clear visualization.

4   Conclusion

In this paper, we proposed a novel 3D multi-scale and dropout modality learning method for IVDs localization and segmentation from multi-modality images. Experimental results on the challenge demonstrated the advantage of our proposed method, which is inherently general and can be applied in other multi-modality image segmentation tasks. Future work includes shape regression based methods to further improve the performance and applying our method on larger dataset.

References

1. http://ivdm3seg.weebly.com
2. Ben Ayed, I., Punithakumar, K., Garvin, G., Romano, W., Li, S.: Graph cuts with invariant object-interaction priors: application to intervertebral disc segmentation. In: Székely, G., Hahn, H.K. (eds.) IPMI 2011. LNCS, vol. 6801, pp. 221–232. Springer, Heidelberg (2011). doi:10.1007/978-3-642-22092-0_19
3. Cai, Y., Landis, M., Laidley, D.T., Kornecki, A., Lum, A., Li, S.: Multi-modal vertebrae recognition using transformed deep convolution network. Comput. Med. Imaging Graph. **51**, 11–19 (2016)
4. Chen, C., Belavy, D., Yu, W., Chu, C., Armbrecht, G., Bansmann, M., Felsenberg, D., Zheng, G.: Localization and segmentation of 3D intervertebral discs in mr images by data driven estimation. IEEE Trans. Med. Imaging **34**(8), 1719–1729 (2015)
5. Chen, H., Dou, Q., Wang, X., Qin, J., Cheng, J.C.Y., Heng, P.-A.: 3D fully convolutional networks for intervertebral disc localization and segmentation. In: Zheng, G., Liao, H., Jannin, P., Cattin, P., Lee, S.-L. (eds.) MIAR 2016. LNCS, vol. 9805, pp. 375–382. Springer, Cham (2016). doi:10.1007/978-3-319-43775-0_34
6. Chen, H., Dou, Q., Yu, L., Heng, P.A.: VoxResNet: deep voxelwise residual networks for volumetric brain segmentation. arXiv preprint arXiv:1608.05895 (2016)
7. Chen, H., Shen, C., Qin, J., Ni, D., Shi, L., Cheng, J.C.Y., Heng, P.-A.: Automatic localization and identification of vertebrae in spine CT via a joint learning model with deep neural networks. In: Navab, N., Hornegger, J., Wells, W.M., Frangi, A.F. (eds.) MICCAI 2015. LNCS, vol. 9349, pp. 515–522. Springer, Cham (2015). doi:10.1007/978-3-319-24553-9_63
8. Chevrefils, C., Chériet, F., Grimard, G., Aubin, C.-E.: Watershed segmentation of intervertebral disk and spinal canal from MRI images. In: Kamel, M., Campilho, A. (eds.) ICIAR 2007. LNCS, vol. 4633, pp. 1017–1027. Springer, Heidelberg (2007). doi:10.1007/978-3-540-74260-9_90
9. Hinton, G.E., Srivastava, N., Krizhevsky, A., Sutskever, I., Salakhutdinov, R.R.: Improving neural networks by preventing co-adaptation of feature detectors. arXiv preprint arXiv:1207.0580 (2012)
10. Jamaludin, A., Kadir, T., Zisserman, A.: SpineNet: automatically pinpointing classification evidence in spinal MRIs. In: Ourselin, S., Joskowicz, L., Sabuncu, M.R., Unal, G., Wells, W. (eds.) MICCAI 2016. LNCS, vol. 9901, pp. 166–175. Springer, Cham (2016). doi:10.1007/978-3-319-46723-8_20
11. Kamnitsas, K., Chen, L., Ledig, C., Rueckert, D., Glocker, B.: Multi-scale 3D convolutional neural networks for lesion segmentation in brain MRI. Ischemic Stroke Lesion Segmen. 13 (2015)

12. Law, M.W., Tay, K., Leung, A., Garvin, G.J., Li, S.: Intervertebral disc segmentation in MR images using anisotropic oriented flux. Med. Image Anal. **17**(1), 43–61 (2013)

13. Srivastava, N., Hinton, G.E., Krizhevsky, A., Sutskever, I., Salakhutdinov, R.: Dropout: a simple way to prevent neural networks from overfitting. J. Mach. Learn. Res. **15**(1), 1929–1958 (2014)

14. Wang, Z., Zhen, X., Tay, K., Osman, S., Romano, W., Li, S.: Regression segmentation for spinal images. IEEE Trans. Med. Imaging **34**(8), 1640–1648 (2015)

15. Zhang, W., Li, R., Deng, H., Wang, L., Lin, W., Ji, S., Shen, D.: Deep convolutional neural networks for multi-modality isointense infant brain image segmentation. NeuroImage **108**, 214–224 (2015)

Fully Automatic Localization and Segmentation of Intervertebral Disc from 3D Multi-modality MR Images by Regression Forest and CNN

Xing Ji[1], Guoyan Zheng[2], Li Liu[1], and Dong Ni[1($\boxtimes$)]

[1] School of Biomedical Engineering, Shenzhen University, Shenzhen, China
nidong@szu.edu.cn
[2] Institute for Surgical Technology and Biomechanics,
University of Bern, Bern, Switzerland
guoyan.zheng@istb.unibe.ch

Abstract. In this paper, we propose a fully automatic framework to localize and segment intervertebral discs (IVDs) from 3D Multi-modality MR Images. Random forest regression is employed to coarsely localize the IVD. Then IVDs are segmented sequentially by training the specific convolutional neural network (CNN) classifier for each IVD. We compared the performance using single- and multi-modality images. Evaluated on the MICCAI 2016 IVD on-site challenge datasets, our method achieved a mean localization distance of 0.64 mm and a mean Dice overlap coefficient of 90.8%. The results show that our method is robust and comparable with state-of-the-art methods.

1 Introduction

Intervertebral disc (IVD) degeneration is a major cause for chronic back pain and function incapacity [1]. The accurate localization and segmentation of IVD region is of great significance for the follow-up treatment and diagnosis of disc disease. Recently, Magnetic Resonance (MR) Imaging (MRI) has become a very useful tool for the diagnosis of IVD disease for its advantages of non-invasiveness, no radiation exposure and offering good soft tissue contrast [2]. In clinical practice, radiologists usually localize and segment IVDs manually for the quantitative diagnosis of disc pathology (See Fig. 1) [3]. However, this progress is time-consuming and experience-dependent, which often leads to significant inter-observer diagnosis variations [4]. Therefore automatic methods for IVD localization and segmentation may help to improve diagnostic efficiency and decrease inter-observer variability.

In the literature, a number of methods have been proposed for the localization and segmentation of the IVDs from MR images [5–8]. There exist methods based on regression forests [5], atlas registration [6], graph cut [7], template matching and statistical shape model [8]. Recently, machine learning-based methods have been adopted for solving the challenging problem. Chen et al. [4] proposed a unified data-driven regression and classification framework to tackle the

© Springer International Publishing AG 2016
J. Yao et al. (Eds.): CSI 2016, LNCS 10182, pp. 92–101, 2016.
DOI: 10.1007/978-3-319-55050-3_9

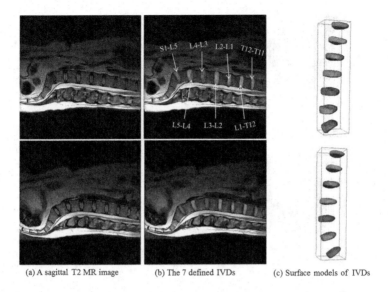

(a) A sagittal T2 MR image   (b) The 7 defined IVDs   (c) Surface models of IVDs

Fig. 1. Manual segmentation of 7 IVD regions from T2-weighted MR images.

problem of localization and segmentation of IVDs from T2-weighted MR data. Wang et al. [9] addressed the segmentation of multiple anatomic structures from multi-modality images via a sparse kernel machines-based regression. In previous learning-based methods, typically only one classifier was trained to segment all IVDs from MR images. However, it may affect the classification performance due to the large appearance variations of different IVDs.

In this study, our task is to automatically locate and segment seven defined IVDs from each set of 3D multi-modality MR images provided by the MICCAI 2016 IVD challenge organizers. We propose a novel learning-based framework for both localization and segmentation tasks. Random forest regression [10] is first employed to coarsely localize the S1-L5 IVD. Then seven IVDs are segmented sequentially from the S1-L5 IVD to T12-T11 IVD by training one convolutional neural network (CNN) [11] classifier for each IVD. The current IVD to be segmented is coarsely localized by the mean shape model based on the locations of the segmented IVDs.

The paper is organized as follows. In Sect. 2, we will describe the proposed architecture and algorithm. The application to the MICCAI 2016 IVD segmentation challenge dataset will be presented in Sect. 3, and we conclude with a discussion in Sect. 4.

2   Methods

The flowchart of the proposed learning framework is shown in Fig. 2. Compared with other IVDs, the S1-L5 IVD is located at the bottom and its appearance is the most discriminative due to the curved shape of the IVDs. We first coarsely

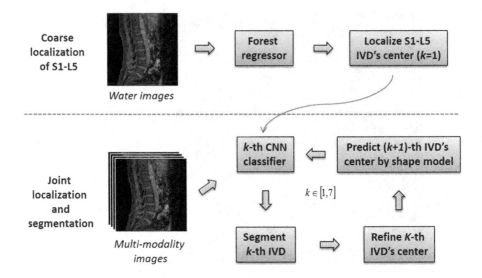

Fig. 2. A schematic view of the workflow for the present method.

localize the center of the S1-L5 IVD ($k = 1$) by training the random forest regressor [10]. Next, we train the k-th ($k \in [1, 7]$) CNN classifier to segment the k-th IVD sequentially. After segmentation, the center of the k-th IVD is refined accordingly. Then the center of the $(k + 1)$-th IVD is predicted by the mean shape model and previously segmented IVDs for accurate segmentation.

2.1   Coarse Localization of the S1-L5 IVD

Random forest [12] is an ensemble learning technique that has been widely applied to a lot of medical image analysis applications with promising performances. This learning algorithm can effectively avoid over-fitting problem with good generalization capability [12]. We employ the forest regression technique [10] to coarsely localize the S1-L5 IVD. The location of the S1-L5 IVD will be used for its accurate segmentation and predicting other IVDs' locations. The parameters of the random forest we set in this study are shown in Table 1.

Table 1. Parameters used in our random forest model

Parameters	Values
No. of sample	16000
No. of feature	200
No. of tree	10
Max depth of each tree	15
Min Leaf number	5

The training and testing progress of the regression model is shown in Fig. 3. We randomly sample a set of 3D image patches around the S1-L5 IVD's center from water images. The 3D random Haar filter [10] is used for computing the visual feature response of each patch. The displacement of each patch to the S1-L5 IVD's center is also computed. Once we obtained the feature matrix and the displacement matrix, we employed the random forest to train the regression model. On the testing phase, given an unseen MR image, the trained regressor was used to predict each voxel's displacement to the target. The voting map is then obtained for the target by adopting the voting strategy in [10] on the displacement maps. Finally, the center of the S1-L5 IVD can be identified by searching the most votes in its voting map.

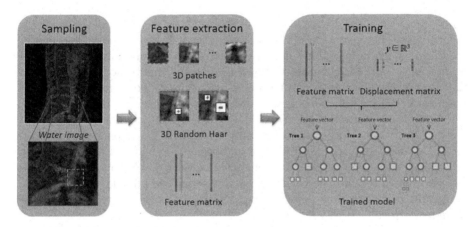

Fig. 3. Illustration of the regression model training. Red points on water image represent centers of sampling patches. 3D Random Haar is used to extract the feature vector of each patch and random forest is used to train our regression model.

2.2 Building Mean Shape Model of IVDs

Our proposed learning framework aims at accurately segmenting each IVD sequentially. Hence, the coarse localization of each IVD is a prerequisite for the following segmentation. In this regard, the mean IVD shape model is constructed for the coarse localization of IVDs. By observing that the shape variance of the curve connecting the centers of seven IVDs is relatively low, we build the shape model by simply averaging the coordinates of each IVD's center of all training data sets (Fig. 4). It is worth noting that the S5-L1 IVD is used as the origin to compute the relative spatial relationship among seven IVDs.

2.3 Accurate Localization and Segmentation of IVDs

Recently, CNN has achieved great success in various medical applications [13–15]. In this study, we trained seven CNN classifiers to segment IVDs

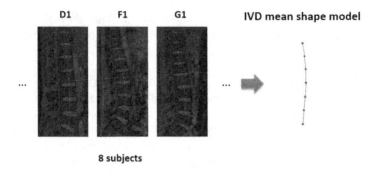

D1   F1   G1   **IVD mean shape model**

...   ...

8 subjects

Fig. 4. The mean IVD shape model.

sequentially. The advantage is that the classifier will become more specific for segmenting each IVD. Table 2 lists the architecture of our CNNs implemented using Caffe [16]. Four channels are used to represent multi-modality images in the input layer. The activation function in our CNNs is chosen to be the retified linear unit (ReLU), which has been shown to expedite the training of CNN [11]. The optimization of our CNNs was done using mini-batch stochastic gradient descent algorithm. Moreover, considering the relative small regions of interest for IVDs when compared with background region, we adopted following patch sampling strategy during the training stage: for each voxel inside the IVDs, we sample a patch around the voxel; for each voxel at the boundary of the IVDs, we sample twice the same patch around the voxel to place more weight on the boundary voxels.

Table 2. Architecture of our CNN model (Conv: convolution, Pool: pooling, FC: fully connected)

Layer	Kernel size/stride	Output size	Feature maps
Input	−/−	20×20	4
Conv1	$5 \times 5/1$	16×16	128
Pool1	$2 \times 2/2$	8×8	128
Conv2	$3 \times 3/1$	8×8	128
Pool2	$2 \times 2/2$	4×4	128
FC	−/−	1×1	512
Softmax	−/−	1×1	2

Once the CNN models are trained, the probability map of the S1-L5 IVD was first obtained using its CNN within the local region detected by the regression model. In practice, multiple regions may be classified as candidates from backgrounds. In this study, we choose the region nearest to the coarsely localized center as the segmentation mask. Then, the center of the current IVD is refined using the segmentation result. For the next IVD to be segmented, we make use of the mean shape model and refined IVDs' centers to get its coarse localization and segment it again until all IVDs are segmented. The detailed progress is shown in Fig. 5.

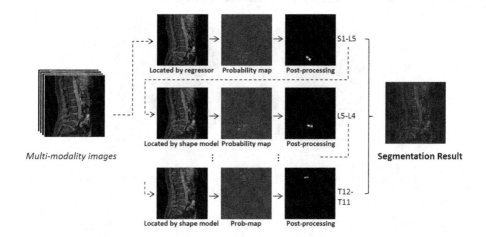

Fig. 5. Localization and segmentation of IVDs using trained CNN models.

3   Experiments and Results

3.1   Materials

The training data provided by the MICCAI 2016 IVD challenge organizers consist of 8 sets of multi-modality MR (M^3) images (Denoted as A1, B1, ... H1 for convenience) and the associated ground truth segmentation. Each set of M^3 images include four aligned 3D images: in-phase, opposed-phase, fat and water images (See Fig. 6). The resolution of all images are $2 \times 1.25 \times 1.25\,\mathrm{m}^3$. There are 2 sets of M^3 images released to verify the developed system before the on-site challenge. In the on-site challenge, 6 more datasets were released to evaluate our proposed method.

3.2   Evaluation Metrics

The metrics introduced in the MICCAI 2016 IVD segmentation challenge are used here to evaluate the performance of our methods. The evaluation metrics for IVD localization include mean localization distance (MLD) with standard deviation (SD) and successful detection rate or percentage P_t of IVD center localized with various ranges of accuracy ($t = 2.0\,\mathrm{mm}$, $4.0\,\mathrm{mm}$ and $6.0\,\mathrm{mm}$). If the absolute difference between the localized IVD center and the ground truth center is no greater than t mm, the localization of this IVD is considered as an

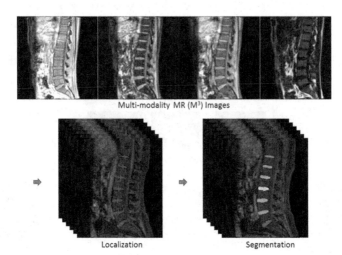

Fig. 6. Multi-modality MR images and associated ground-truth.

accurate detection; otherwise, it is considered as a false localization. The evaluation metrics on IVD segmentation include the mean Dice overlap coefficients (MDOC) with standard deviation (SDDOC) between the ground truth segmentation and the automated segmentation, as well as the mean average absolute surface distance (MASD) with standard deviation (SDASD) between the surface models extracted from the ground truth segmentation and those extracted from the automated segmentation.

3.3 Evaluation on Off-site Challenge Datasets

The qualitative segmentation results of off-site challenge datasets by our method are shown in Fig. 7. It demonstrates that our segmentation results are consistent with the ground-truth. Table 3 shows the segmentation results with the leave-one-out cross validation on training data. We computed the Dice overlap coefficient to evaluate our method. We achieved a MDOC of 90.4%. The results on 2 validation datasets were evaluated by the challenge organizers (Tables 4 and 5). We achieved a MLD of 0.68 mm for localization and a MDOC of 90.9% for segmentation.

Table 3. Segmentation results with leave-one-out cross validation

Dice overlap coefficient (%)								
A1	B1	C1	D1	E1	F1	G1	H1	MDOC ± SDDOC
90.5	89.8	91.2	91.8	90.4	90.1	90.2	88.8	90.4 ± 2.5

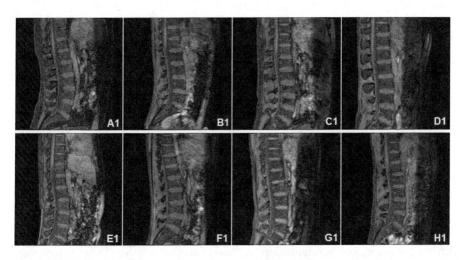

Fig. 7. Examples of segmentation visualized on our methods with leave-one-out cross validation. (Red: segmentation results by our methods; Green: ground-truth). (Color figure online)

Table 4. Localization results on 2 validation datasets

MLD	SD	P_2	P_4	P_6
0.68 mm	0.38 mm	100.0%	100.0%	100.0%

We further compared the segmentation results using multi-modality (Multi) images and single-modality images (denoted as Fat, Inn, Opp and Wat, respectively) in Table 6. It can be observed that we achieved the best result on multi-modality images. The results on opposed-phase and water images are comparable to the best result.

3.4 Evaluation on On-site Challenge Datasets

The quantitative localization and segmentation results of on-site challenge datasets by our method are shown in Table 7. We achieved a MLD of 0.64 mm for localization and a MDOC of 90.8% for segmentation. The results are highly consistent with previous results on training and validation datasets.

Table 5. Segmentation results on 2 validation datasets

MDOC	SDDOC	MASD	SDASD
90.9%	1.7%	1.04 mm	0.03 mm

Table 6. Comparison of segmentation results using multi- and single-modality images

MDOC (%)				
Multi	Fat	Inn	Opp	Wat
90.4 ± 2.5	87.2 ± 3.7	80.5 ± 8.6	90.2 ± 2.2	90.3 ± 2.4

Table 7. Localization and segmentation results with the 6 on-site test datasets

MLD	SD	MDOC	SDDOC	MASD	SDASD
0.64 mm	0.50 mm	90.8%	3.9%	1.07 mm	0.17 mm

3.5   Computation Time

Different from global segmentation methods, we first localize IVDs before segmentation. Our method can save much time of computing on background voxels. Generally, for a set of multi-modality MR images of $36 \times 256 \times 256$, it takes about 30 s to obtain final results including 5 s for localization and 25 s for segmentation using a standard PC with a 2.60 GHz Intel (R) Xeon (R) E5-2650 V2 CPU and a NVIDIA Tesla K80 GPU. The fast speed makes our system promising for clinical application.

4   Conclusions

In this paper, we propose a novel learning framework for fully automatic localization and segmentation of IVDs from multi-modality MR images. Random forest and CNN are employed for localization and segmentation tasks, respectively. Evaluation on the MICCAI 2016 IVD challenge datasets shows that our method is robust and comparable with state-of-the-art methods. In addition, we investigated the influence of modality information on the performance. Future work will include further refining the segmentation on the IVD boundaries and testing our method on pathological cases.

References

1. Modic, M.T., Ross, J.S.: Lumbar degenerative disk disease. Radiology **245**(1), 43–61 (2007)
2. Parizel, P.M., Van Goethem, W.M.: Degenerative disc disease. Alphascript Publ. **79**(1), 127–156 (2006)
3. Niemelainen, R., Videman, T., Dhillon, S.S., Batti, M.C.: Quantitative measurement of intervertebral disc signal using MRI. Clin. Radiol. **63**(3), 252–255 (2008)
4. Chen, C., Belavy, D., Yu, W., Chu, C., Armbrecht, G., Bansmann, M., Felsenberg, D., Zheng, G.: Localization and segmentation of 3D intervertebral discs in MR images by data driven estimation. IEEE Trans. Med. Imaging **34**(8), 1 (2015)

5. Glocker, B., Feulner, J., Criminisi, A., Haynor, D.R., Konukoglu, E.: Automatic localization and identification of vertebrae in arbitrary field-of-view CT scans. In: Ayache, N., Delingette, H., Golland, P., Mori, K. (eds.) MICCAI 2012. LNCS, vol. 7512, pp. 590–598. Springer, Heidelberg (2012). doi:10.1007/978-3-642-33454-2_73

6. Michopoulou, S.K., Costaridou, L., Panagiotopoulos, E., Speller, R.: Atlas-based segmentation of degenerated lumbar intervertebral discs from MR images of the spine. IEEE Trans. Biomed. Eng. **56**(9), 2225–2231 (2009)

7. Ben Ayed, I., Punithakumar, K., Garvin, G., Romano, W., Li, S.: Graph cuts with invariant object-interaction priors: application to intervertebral disc segmentation. In: Székely, G., Hahn, H.K. (eds.) IPMI 2011. LNCS, vol. 6801, pp. 221–232. Springer, Heidelberg (2011). doi:10.1007/978-3-642-22092-0_19

8. Neubert, A., Fripp, J., Shen, K., Salvado, O., Schwarz, R., Lauer, L., Engstrom, C., Crozier, S.: Automated 3D segmentation of vertebral bodies and intervertebral discs from MRI. In: International Conference on Digital Image Computing Techniques and Applications, pp. 19–24 (2011)

9. Wang, Z., Zhen, X., Tay, K., Osman, S., Romano, W., Li, S.: Regression segmentation for M^3 spinal images. IEEE Trans. Med. Imaging **34**(9), 1989–1989 (2014)

10. Gao, Y., Shen, D.: Context-Aware anatomical landmark detection: application to deformable model initialization in prostate CT images. In: Wu, G., Zhang, D., Zhou, L. (eds.) MLMI 2014. LNCS, vol. 8679, pp. 165–173. Springer, Cham (2014). doi:10.1007/978-3-319-10581-9_21

11. Krizhevsky, A., Sutskever, I., Hinton, G.E.: Imagenet classification with deep convolutional neural networks. In: International Conference on Neural Information Processing Systems, pp. 1097–1105 (2012)

12. Breiman, L.: Random forests. Mach. Learn. **45**(1), 5–32 (2001)

13. Prasoon, A., Petersen, K., Igel, C., Lauze, F., Dam, E., Nielsen, M.: Deep feature learning for knee cartilage segmentation using a triplanar convolutional neural network. In: Mori, K., Sakuma, I., Sato, Y., Barillot, C., Navab, N. (eds.) MICCAI 2013. LNCS, vol. 8150, pp. 246–253. Springer, Heidelberg (2013). doi:10.1007/978-3-642-40763-5_31

14. Roth, H.R., et al.: A new 2.5D representation for lymph node detection using random sets of deep convolutional neural network observations. In: Golland, P., Hata, N., Barillot, C., Hornegger, J., Howe, R. (eds.) MICCAI 2014. LNCS, vol. 8673, pp. 520–527. Springer, Cham (2014). doi:10.1007/978-3-319-10404-1_65

15. Roth, H.R., Yao, J., Le, L., Stieger, J., Burns, J.E., Summers, R.M.: Detection of sclerotic spine metastases via random aggregation of deep convolutional neural network classifications. In: Yao, J., Glocker, B., Klinder, T., Li, S. (eds.) Recent Advances in Computational Methods and Clinical Applications for Spine Imaging. LNCVB, vol. 20, pp. 3–12. Springer, Cham (2015)

16. Jia, Y., Shelhamer, E., Donahue, J., Karayev, S., Long, J.: Caffe: convolutional architecture for fast feature embedding. Eprint ArXiv, pp. 675–678 (2014)

Computer Aided Diagnosis and
Intervention

Manual and Computer-Assisted Pedicle Screw Placement Plans: A Quantitative Comparison

Dejan Knez[1]([✉]), Janez Mohar[2], Robert J. Cirman[2], Boštjan Likar[1],
Franjo Pernuš[1], and Tomaž Vrtovec[1]

[1] Faculty of Electrical Engineering, University of Ljubljana, Ljubljana, Slovenia
{dejan.knez,bostjan.likar,franjo.pernus,tomaz.vrtovec}@fe.uni-lj.si
[2] Valdoltra Orthopaedic Hospital, Ankaran, Slovenia
{janez.mohar,robertjanez.cirman}@ob-valdoltra.si

Abstract. In this paper, we present a quantitative comparison of manual and computer-assisted preoperative pedicle screw placement plans, obtained from three-dimensional (3D) computed tomography (CT) images of 17 patients with thoracic spinal deformities. Manual planning was performed by two spine surgeons by means of a dedicated software for planning of surgical procedures, while computer-assisted planning was based on automated 3D segmentation and modeling of vertebral structures from CT images, and automated modeling of the pedicle screw in 3D with maximization of the screw fastening strength. The analysis of the size (diameter and length) and insertion trajectory (pedicle crossing point, sagittal and axial inclinations) for 316 pedicle screws revealed a statistically significant difference in the screw size and insertion trajectory. However, computer-assisted planning did not propose narrower and shorter screws, which was reflected through a higher normalized screw fastening strength.

1 Introduction

Vertebral fixation by pedicle screw placement is one of the most widely used stabilization techniques in spine surgery [1–3]. It is used for treating various pathological conditions of the spine, such as deformities, tumors and fractures, as well as for other degenerations that cause spinal instability. The procedure is based on anchoring two (or more) vertebrae to each other by inserting screws through vertebral pedicles from the posterior side so that they reach the interior of the vertebral body, and then bilaterally (i.e. on each side of the vertebra) attaching a stabilizing rod to the exterior part of the screws [4]. As such, the procedure is considered complex and technically demanding with a steep learning curve, because the visibility of anatomical structures is limited during the surgery, and therefore a mental conceptualization of three-dimensional (3D) spinal anatomical structures that are hidden from direct view is required.

Although pedicles are, from the biomechanical point of view, the hardest part of the vertebra, their narrow anatomical shape poses a risk of injury to the spinal cord, spinal nerve roots, vascular structures and vital organs that can

© Springer International Publishing AG 2016
J. Yao et al. (Eds.): CSI 2016, LNCS 10182, pp. 105–115, 2016.
DOI: 10.1007/978-3-319-55050-3_10

be caused by pedicle wall breakthrough or other damage in the case of pedicle screw misplacement [5]. For a safe pedicle screw placement, the spine surgeon has to perform proper surgery planning by taking into account the morphometry (shape and structure) of pedicles and vertebral bodies, and choosing the appropriate size (i.e. diameter and length) and insertion trajectory (i.e. entry point and inclinations) of each pedicle screw, which has proved valuable for reducing the risk of screw misplacement. However, the accuracy of pedicle screw placement is directly related to the expertise of the spine surgeon, and therefore several methods for computer-assisted surgery (CAS) have been developed, where intraoperative navigation based on markers and adequate software is used to visualize and track surgical instruments relative to the patient anatomy [6]. The advantages of CAS are reflected in a less invasive surgery, higher accuracy of pedicle screw placement, lower costs from the point of view of screw misplacement, and in allowing simulations, which help spine surgeons to gain experience. On the other hand, the disadvantages of CAS are variable patient positioning during the procedure, variable accuracy of surgical instrument tracking and a relatively high cost of the system.

Preoperative surgery planning based on 3D images of the spine, which are usually acquired by the computed tomography (CT) imaging technique [7] that provides an accurate insight into the anatomical structure and shape of the spine, has become essential for pedicle screw placement. In this paper, we present a quantitative comparison of manual and computer-assisted pedicle screw placement plans, obtained from CT images with thoracic spinal deformities.

2 Methodology

2.1 Manual Pedicle Screw Placement Plans

Manual planning was performed by means of 3D visualization of the spine anatomy from CT images and by using a dedicated medical software for trauma and orthopedic surgery planning (EBS, Ekliptik d.o.o., Ljubljana, Slovenia), which was divided into three steps. In the first step, the spine was segmented by simple thresholding of CT image intensities to obtain the corresponding 3D triangular mesh model, which enabled 3D visualization of the spine (Fig. 1(a)). In the second step, manual labeling of vertebrae (segments T1–T12) was first performed based on the visualized 3D spine model and the CT image, and then the initial pedicle screw insertion trajectory was determined by placing a 3D pedicle screw model into the 3D spine model and the CT image, and through its manipulation the virtual screw entry point into each observed pedicle and the virtual screw exit point from the corresponding vertebral body were identified (Fig. 1(b)). The final pedicle screw trajectory (i.e. entry point and inclinations) was determined in the third step by moving the pedicle screw virtual entry and exit points within the oblique cross-section, defined by the initial insertion trajectory and the normal to the current view in the 3D space (Fig. 1(c)), while the final pedicle screw size (i.e. diameter and length) was determined by a thorough analysis of the anatomy of the observed pedicle and the corresponding vertebral

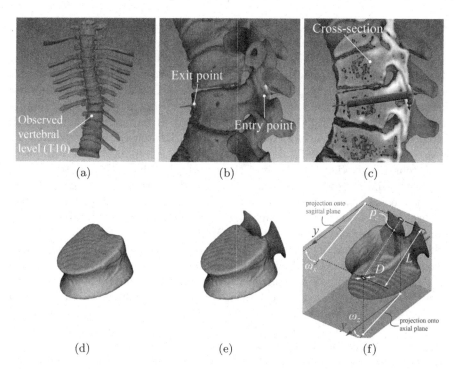

Fig. 1. Manual ((a)–(c)) and computer-assisted ((d)–(f)) planning of the pedicle screw size and insertion trajectory. (a) The 3D triangular mesh model of the spine, obtained by thresholding the CT image. (b) Determination of the virtual entry point into the pedicle and the virtual exit point from the vertebral body. (c) Determination of the final pedicle screw trajectory within the predefined cross-section. (d) The 3D model of the vertebral body, representing its segmentation from the CT image. (e) The 3D models of the left and right pedicle, representing their segmentations from the CT image. (f) The 3D models of the screws through the left and right pedicle.

body. The resulting pedicle screw sizes and insertion trajectories had to provide a high level of safety for their insertion (i.e. preventing pedicle and/or vertebral body wall breakthrough) considering the maximal allowable screw diameters and lengths, which were consistent with the usage and availability of pedicle screws in clinical practice, i.e. the screw diameter was determined by increments of 0.5 mm and the screw length by increments of 5 mm. In the case the pedicle anatomy did not allow a safe insertion of the screw with a diameter of at least 3 mm (the smallest available diameter), the screw was excluded from the preoperative plan.

2.2   Computer-Assisted Pedicle Screw Placement Plans

Computer-assisted planning was performed by means of the method proposed by Knez et al. [8] that first automatically segments the vertebral bodies and pedicles from the CT image by 3D geometrical modeling, and then automatically determines the size and insertion trajectory of each pedicle screw by modeling the screw in 3D and maximization of its fastening strength.

The initial 3D vertebral body model is represented in the form of an elliptical cylinder, which is then deformed by introducing additional shape parameters and aligned to the observed vertebral body in the CT image by maximizing the similarity between the 3D model and the corresponding anatomy. The final 3D vertebral body model (Fig. 1(d)) is represented by 31 parameters, out of which six represent its position and orientation in the 3D image, three represent its 3D size and the remaining 22 represent specific 3D anatomical deformations of the vertebral body (i.e. the shape of the vertebral body at the location of the left pedicle, right pedicle, vertebral foramen and anterior part of the vertebral body; the concavity of the vertebral body wall at its anterior part and at the vertebral foramen; the concavity and sagittal inclinations of vertebral endplates; the increasing size and torsion of the vertebral body).

The obtained final 3D vertebral body model is used to define the location of the initial 3D pedicle model, which is also represented in the form of an elliptical cylinder, and is then again deformed by introducing additional shape parameters and aligned to the observed pedicle in the CT image. The final 3D pedicle model (Fig. 1(e)) is represented by 38 parameters, out of which six represent its position and orientation in the 3D image, three represent its 3D size and the remaining 29 represent specific 3D anatomical deformations of the pedicle (i.e. the pedicle wall concavity at its anterior, posterior, right and left parts; the shape of the pedicle at its anterior, posterior, right and left tails; the teardrop and kidney shape of the pedicle cross-section; the torsion of the pedicle).

Both the obtained final 3D vertebral body and pedicle models are then used to model the corresponding pedicle screw in the form of a circular cylinder (Fig. 1(f)). The pedicle screw size (i.e. diameter and length) is determined from the geometrical properties of the corresponding anatomy, represented by the 3D vertebral body and pedicle models, i.e. its diameter is determined as 70% of the narrowest pedicle diameter [9], while its length as 80% of the anteroposterior size of the vertebral body [2]. On the other hand, the pedicle screw insertion trajectory (i.e. entry point and inclination angles) is determined from the structural properties of the corresponding anatomy by maximizing the screw fastening strength, defined as the sum of the underlying CT image intensities. It was shown that CT image intensities as well as the screw pull-out strength correlate with the corresponding bone mineral density (BMD) [2,10], and consequently the screw fastening strength is strongly related with its pull-out strength [11], which represents one of the most important biomechanical properties for pedicle screw placement. For the computation of the fastening strength, only CT image intensities within a relatively small neighborhood of the 3D pedicle screw surface, representing the surrounding volume around the screw thread, are taken into account and additionally weighted according to the distance from the longitudinal pedicle axis in order to reduce the potential impact of higher intensities close to the pedicle screw surface. Moreover, the fastening strength is normalized with the surrounding volume around the screw thread to avoid the influence of different

Table 1. The number of the observed vertebral bodies (VBs) and pedicle screws for each vertebral segment (T1–T12) and patient's diagnosis, i.e. adolescent idiopathic scoliosis (AIS) and Scheuermann's kyphosis (SK) in CT images of the thoracic spine from 17 patients.

Segment	T1	T2	T3	T4	T5	T6	T7	T8	T9	T10	T11	T12	All
No. of VBs	3	10	12	13	14	15	14	17	16	17	17	16	**164**
AIS	3	8	10	11	11	12	11	13	13	13	13	12	**130**
SK	0	2	2	2	3	3	3	4	3	4	4	4	**34**
No. of screws	6	20	22	23	27	28	27	33	31	33	34	32	**316**
AIS	6	16	19	19	22	22	21	25	25	25	26	24	**250**
SK	0	4	3	4	5	6	6	8	6	8	8	8	**66**

screw sizes. Besides structural, also geometrical properties of the corresponding anatomy are taken into account for the determination of the pedicle screw insertion trajectory, i.e. each screw has to be completely inside the corresponding 3D vertebral body and pedicle models, and the intersection point between the screw insertion trajectory and the plane of sagittal symmetry of the vertebral body has to be outside the corresponding 3D vertebral body model. Therefore, computer-assisted planning automatically determines the optimal pedicle screw size and insertion trajectory with the highest possible screw fastening strength according to the structure of the observed vertebra while limiting both the screw size and insertion trajectory by the anatomical shape of the observed pedicle and the corresponding vertebral body.

3   Results

Quantitative comparison of pedicle screw placement plans was performed for 17 patients (males: 12; females: 5; mean age: 17.6 years; age range: 12–14 years) with thoracic spinal deformities (adolescent idiopathic scoliosis: 13; Scheuermann's kyphosis: 4). All patients were appointed for the pedicle screw placement surgery at Orthopaedic Hospital Valdoltra, Slovenia, between 2013 and 2016. For the purpose of surgery planning, preoperative CT images of the thoracic spine were acquired, usually between the first (T1) and last (T12) thoracic vertebra (GE LightSpeed VTC; pixel size: 0.25–0.38 mm; slice thickness: 0.6 mm). For all patients, a spine surgeon manually defined preoperative pedicle screw placement plans that were used to construct patient-specific drill guides, which were intraoperatively laid over the visible part of the spine. Pedicle screws with predefined sizes were then placed along these guides, which defined their insertion trajectory.

For the purpose of quantitative comparison, manual planning was additionally performed by two experienced spine surgeons, who independently determined pedicle screw sizes and insertion trajectories as described in Sect. 2.1 (first surgeon: M_1; second surgeon: M_2), while computer-assisted planning was performed by the automated method of Knez et al. [8] as described in Sect. 2.2 (computer: C) with an estimated modeling accuracy of 0.39 ± 0.31 mm for vertebral bodies and 0.31 ± 0.25 mm for pedicles [8] in terms of the mean absolute difference (MAD) and corresponding standard deviation (SD). The results were obtained for CT images of all 17 patients, where the parameters for 316 pedicle screws through 158 left and 158 right pedicles of 164 vertebral bodies were determined (Table 1). The obtained pedicle screw parameters consisted of the screw size (i.e. diameter D and length L), insertion trajectory (i.e. pedicle crossing point $p_c = [x_c, y_c, z_c]$, sagittal ω_x and axial ω_z inclinations) and normalized fastening strength F_n (Fig. 1(f)). For each parameter of the pedicle screw, three values (M_1, M_2 and C) were independently obtained and further used for quantitative comparison and statistical analysis (Student t-test; significance level: $p < 0.05$). The results are presented in Tables 2 and 3, while Fig. 2 shows examples of the obtained pedicle screw placement plans.

The quantitative comparison of the obtained pedicle screw sizes and insertion trajectories between manual plans M_1 and manual plans M_2 (Tables 2 and 3)

Table 2. Quantitative comparison of manual (M_1 and M_2) and computer-assisted (C) preoperative planning of the size (i.e. diameter D and length L) and insertion trajectory (i.e. pedicle crossing point p_c, sagittal inclination angle ω_x and axial inclination angle ω_z) for 316 pedicle screws in CT images of the thoracic spine (segments T1–T12) from 17 patients in terms of the mean absolute difference (MAD) and corresponding standard deviation (SD).

Segment	T1	T2	T3	T4	T5	T6	T7	T8	T9	T10	T11	T12	All
$D\{M_1$ vs. $M_2\}$ (mm)	0.8 (0.5)	0.5 (0.5)	0.3 (0.3)	0.2 (0.2)	0.3 (0.4)	0.3 (0.4)	0.3 (0.3)	0.6 (0.5)	0.5 (0.4)	0.6 (0.5)	0.4 (0.4)	0.4 (0.4)	**0.4 (0.4)**
$D\{M_1$ vs. C$\}$ (mm)	1.0 (0.7)	0.6 (0.5)	0.3 (0.4)	0.4 (0.4)	0.3 (0.4)	0.4 (0.4)	0.3 (0.5)	0.6 (0.6)	0.4 (0.4)	0.7 (0.6)	0.8 (0.5)	0.6 (0.4)	**0.5 (0.5)**
$D\{M_2$ vs. C$\}$ (mm)	0.4 (0.4)	0.3 (0.3)	0.4 (0.3)	0.4 (0.3)	0.4 (0.3)	0.4 (0.3)	0.4 (0.4)	0.4 (0.3)	0.4 (0.3)	0.3 (0.3)	0.5 (0.4)	0.5 (0.4)	**0.4 (0.3)**
$L\{M_1$ vs. $M_2\}$ (mm)	1.7 (2.6)	3.0 (3.0)	2.5 (2.6)	3.0 (2.9)	2.0 (3.2)	2.5 (2.5)	2.6 (3.2)	2.8 (2.8)	3.4 (3.3)	2.7 (2.5)	2.6 (3.3)	4.2 (3.4)	**2.9 (3.0)**
$L\{M_1$ vs. C$\}$ (mm)	2.3 (1.9)	3.2 (2.4)	3.7 (2.5)	4.1 (3.2)	2.7 (2.1)	3.4 (4.0)	4.3 (3.9)	4.1 (3.7)	4.5 (3.7)	3.8 (3.5)	3.5 (2.6)	6.7 (3.8)	**4.0 (3.4)**
$L\{M_2$ vs. C$\}$ (mm)	2.0 (1.8)	2.3 (1.5)	4.0 (4.4)	3.3 (3.2)	2.4 (1.5)	3.3 (3.1)	3.0 (2.3)	3.0 (4.0)	4.3 (4.1)	3.7 (3.4)	3.6 (3.0)	5.0 (3.3)	**3.5 (3.3)**
$p_c\{M_1$ vs. $M_2\}$ (mm)	1.2 (0.9)	1.3 (1.0)	1.3 (0.7)	1.4 (0.9)	1.3 (1.0)	1.4 (1.0)	1.4 (1.4)	1.4 (1.1)	1.4 (1.2)	2.0 (1.6)	2.8 (2.2)	2.0 (1.2)	**1.7 (1.4)**
$p_c\{M_1$ vs. C$\}$ (mm)	2.0 (1.1)	1.3 (1.1)	1.5 (1.0)	1.3 (1.0)	1.1 (0.8)	1.2 (0.9)	1.2 (0.9)	1.5 (1.2)	1.4 (0.8)	1.6 (0.9)	2.3 (1.3)	2.1 (1.1)	**1.6 (1.1)**
$p_c\{M_2$ vs. C$\}$ (mm)	1.4 (1.2)	1.3 (1.1)	1.1 (0.7)	1.0 (0.6)	1.3 (1.0)	1.3 (0.7)	1.3 (0.7)	1.4 (0.9)	1.4 (0.9)	1.9 (1.5)	2.1 (1.2)	1.9 (1.4)	**1.5 (1.1)**
$\omega_x\{M_1$ vs. $M_2\}$ (°)	5.3 (2.8)	3.6 (2.9)	3.1 (3.3)	3.9 (3.4)	4.1 (3.3)	3.7 (3.2)	4.3 (3.2)	3.5 (2.8)	3.3 (2.8)	3.7 (2.7)	5.0 (3.7)	3.7 (3.4)	**3.8 (3.2)**
$\omega_x\{M_1$ vs. C$\}$ (°)	18.6 (7.4)	7.7 (6.8)	8.5 (4.0)	8.4 (5.6)	11.3 (6.0)	9.7 (5.9)	10.3 (5.8)	10.5 (4.5)	10.7 (5.7)	12.1 (5.4)	11.7 (6.6)	9.7 (5.9)	**10.4 (5.9)**
$\omega_x\{M_2$ vs. C$\}$ (°)	17.1 (4.3)	7.6 (4.7)	8.6 (3.8)	8.0 (4.4)	10.1 (4.4)	10.1 (5.4)	10.8 (6.0)	10.3 (4.8)	10.2 (4.3)	12.0 (6.3)	13.5 (7.8)	8.9 (5.5)	**10.6 (5.9)**
$\omega_z\{M_1$ vs. $M_2\}$ (°)	3.7 (2.4)	6.9 (3.4)	5.3 (4.2)	3.2 (2.8)	3.7 (2.8)	3.7 (2.9)	4.7 (3.5)	4.3 (3.0)	4.5 (2.8)	4.1 (3.1)	4.0 (3.3)	3.2 (3.0)	**4.2 (3.3)**
$\omega_z\{M_1$ vs. C$\}$ (°)	2.9 (3.0)	7.9 (5.0)	5.6 (3.9)	4.2 (3.0)	4.9 (3.6)	5.3 (4.5)	5.8 (4.5)	5.9 (4.2)	6.1 (3.5)	6.4 (4.0)	5.6 (4.1)	6.2 (4.6)	**5.8 (4.1)**
$\omega_z\{M_2$ vs. C$\}$ (°)	4.0 (3.1)	3.8 (2.9)	4.4 (4.6)	4.1 (2.6)	4.2 (3.1)	4.2 (2.8)	4.7 (3.6)	4.4 (3.0)	4.0 (2.6)	5.0 (3.8)	5.2 (4.3)	5.8 (5.1)	**4.6 (3.6)**

Table 3. Quantitative comparison of manual (M_1 and M_2) and computer-assisted (C) preoperative planning of the normalized fastening strength F_n for 316 pedicle screws in CT images of the thoracic spine (segments T1–T12) from 17 patients in terms of the mean absolute difference (MAD) and corresponding standard deviation (SD).

Segment	T1	T2	T3	T4	T5	T6	T7	T8	T9	T10	T11	T12	All
$F_n\{M_1$ vs. $M_2\}$ (%)	47	19	16	12	12	11	10	8	8	8	10	12	**11**
	(5)	(25)	(22)	(19)	(12)	(16)	(8)	(6)	(7)	(10)	(6)	(16)	**(14)**
$F_n\{M_1$ vs. $C\}$ (%)	11	26	12	18	13	14	15	18	17	18	15	15	**16**
	(10)	(36)	(14)	(32)	(12)	(9)	(15)	(17)	(19)	(23)	(15)	(16)	**(20)**
$F_n\{M_2$ vs. $C\}$ (%)	12	22	14	24	21	20	21	20	10	18	16	16	**19**
	(9)	(44)	(21)	(30)	(19)	(23)	(16)	(19)	(16)	(21)	(12)	(15)	**(22)**

revealed that the differences between M_1 and M_2 are on average 0.4 ± 0.4 mm for diameter D and 2.9 ± 3.0 mm for length L related to the pedicle screw size, 1.7 ± 1.4 mm for pedicle crossing point p_c, $3.8\pm3.2°$ for sagittal inclination ω_x and $4.3\pm3.3°$ for axial inclination ω_z related to the insertion trajectory, and $11\pm14\%$ for normalized screw fastening strength F_n. Statistically significant differences were observed for planning of the pedicle screw size ($p < 0.001$) and inclinations ($p < 0.05$), where, in comparison to M_2, manual planning M_1 proposed narrower ($p < 0.05$) and longer ($p < 0.05$) screws with a smaller corresponding normalized fastening strength ($p < 0.05$). The comparison among both manual plans M_1 and M_2, and computer-assisted plans C (Tables 2 and 3) revealed that the differences between M_1 and C are on average 0.5 ± 0.5 mm for diameter D and 4.0 ± 3.4 mm for length L related to the pedicle screw size, 1.6 ± 1.1 mm for pedicle crossing point p_c, $10.4\pm5.9°$ for sagittal inclination ω_x and $5.8\pm4.1°$ for axial inclination ω_z related to the insertion trajectory, and $16\pm20\%$ for normalized screw fastening strength F_n. The differences between M_2 and C are on average 0.4 ± 0.3 mm for diameter D and 3.5 ± 3.3 mm for length L related to the pedicle screw size, 1.5 ± 1.1 mm for pedicle crossing point p_c, $10.6 \pm 5.9°$ for sagittal inclination ω_x and $4.6 \pm 3.6°$ for axial inclination ω_x related to the insertion trajectory, and $19 \pm 22\%$ for normalized screw fastening strength F_n. Statistically significant differences were observed for planning of the pedicle screw size ($p < 0.001$) and inclinations ($p < 0.05$), where, in comparison to M_1 and M_2, computer-assisted planning C did not propose narrower ($p < 0.05$) and shorter ($p < 0.001$) screws, but the corresponding normalized fastening strength was higher ($p < 0.001$).

4   Discussion

In this paper, we present a quantitative comparison and analysis of manual and computer-assisted preoperative planning of the pedicle screw size and insertion trajectory. Although modern software enables 3D visualization of medical images, navigation through 3D images and manipulation with 3D pedicle screw models, the above described manual planning of the pedicle screw size and insertion trajectory is still a relatively time-consuming procedure. Moreover, by manual planning it is impossible to take into account all parameters, which are

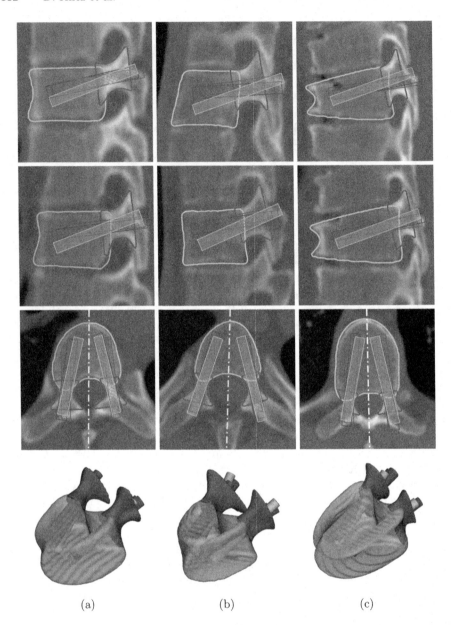

(a)   (b)   (c)

Fig. 2. Manual planning M_1 (in red), manual planning M_2 (in blue) and computer-assisted planning C (in gray) of the pedicle screw size and insertion trajectory for (a) patient 1: segment T7, (b) patient 4: segment T3 and (c) patient 12: segment T10. From top to bottom are displayed the sagittal CT cross-sectional view through the right pedicle, the sagittal CT cross-sectional view through the left pedicle, the axial CT cross-sectional view through both pedicles, and a 3D view. (Color figure online)

important for the insertion of pedicle screws, such as the screw pull-out strength and the corresponding screw fastening strength. On the other hand, computer-assisted planning is a relatively fast procedure, as it can be performed without the presence of a spine surgeon and/or a second observer, while still allowing to perform some eventual manual adjustments or other settings. An important advantage of computer-assisted planning is its repeatability and reliability, because it is based on the optimization of the parameters that are important for pedicle screw placement, i.e. searching for the highest possible screw fastening strength for the observed structure and shape of the vertebral body and pedicle.

The differences between manual plans (M_1 vs. M_2), obtained from two experienced spine surgeons, were on average relatively small, however, surgeon M_1 proposed narrower and longer pedicle screws with a smaller corresponding normalized fastening strength. The size and the related fastening strength of manually planned pedicle screws are consistent with the findings of Chapman et al. [12] and Bianco et al. [13], who reported that the screw pull-out strength is mainly affected and in fact increases by its diameter. However, the pedicle screw length, compared to its diameter, does not largely affect its pull-out strength, which additionally confirms the findings of Hirano et al. [14], who reported that approximately 60% of the pedicle screw pull-out strength is within the pedicle and the remaining 40% is within the vertebral body. The differences between manual and computer-assisted plans (M_1 vs. C and M_2 vs. C) are comparable according to the order of magnitude, which is consistent with previous finding that the differences between both manual plans are relatively small. Furthermore, the average differences between both manual plans and computer-assisted plans (M_1 vs. C and M_2 vs. C) are in most cases relatively small and comparable to the differences between manual plans (M_1 vs. M_2), except for the sagittal inclination of the screw insertion trajectory, where on average higher differences occurred because vertebral morphometry allows a greater range of pedicle screw inclinations in the sagittal plane. As a result, two techniques of pedicle screw insertion are established in clinical practice, i.e. the anatomical technique with the screw insertion trajectory parallel to the longitudinal axis of the pedicle [15], and the straight-forward technique with the screw insertion trajectory parallel to the superior endplate of the vertebral body [16], where a difference of up to 25° in sagittal screw inclinations can occur between both insertion techniques [2]. The average differences in sagittal screw inclinations between the obtained manual and computer-assisted plans are within the above mentioned range (i.e. $10.4 \pm 5.9°$ for M_1 vs. C and $10.6 \pm 5.9°$ for M_2 vs. C), and the analysis of non-absolute differences in sagittal inclinations revealed that computer-assisted plans were more consistent with the anatomical technique, while manual plans were more consistent with the straight-forward technique. The statistical analysis of the obtained results also revealed that, at higher screw fastening strength, computer-assisted plans did not result in narrower and shorter pedicle screws when compared to both manual plans, which is in accordance to the above mentioned findings that the pedicle screw length does not largely influence the screw pull-out strength in comparison to the screw diameter.

Acknowledgements. This work was supported by the Slovenian Research Agency under grants P2-0232, J2-5473, J7-6781 and J2-7118. The authors thank Ekliptik d.o.o., Slovenia, for using EBS for manual preoperative pedicle screw placement planning.

References

1. Tian, N.F., Huang, Q.S., Zhou, P., Zhou, Y., Wu, R.K., Lou, Y., Xu, H.Z.: Pedicle screw insertion accuracy with different assisted methods: a systematic review and meta-analysis of comparative studies. Eur. Spine J. **20**(6), 846–859 (2010)

2. Lehman, R.A., Polly, D.W., Kuklo, T.R., Cunningham, B., Kirk, K.L., Belmont, P.J.: Straight-forward versus anatomic trajectory technique of thoracic pedicle screw fixation: a biomechanical analysis. Spine **28**(18), 2058–2065 (2003)

3. Lee, C.S., Park, S.A., Hwang, C.J., Kim, D.J., Lee, W.J., Kim, Y.T., Lee, M.Y., Yoon, S.J., Lee, D.H.: A novel method of screw placement for extremely small thoracic pedicles in scoliosis. Spine **36**(16), E1112–E1116 (2011)

4. Koktekir, E., Ceylan, D., Tatarli, N., Karabagli, H., Recber, F., Akdemir, G.: Accuracy of fluoroscopically-assisted pedicle screw placement: analysis of 1,218 screws in 198 patients. Spine J. **14**(8), 1702–1708 (2014)

5. Cho, S.K., Skovrlj, B., Lu, Y., Caridi, J.M., Lenke, L.G.: The effect of increasing pedicle screw size on thoracic spinal canal dimensions: an anatomic study. Spine **39**(20), E1195–E1200 (2014)

6. Kleck, C.J., Cullilmore, I., LaFleur, M., Lindley, E., Rentschler, M.E., Burger, E.L., Cain, C.M.J., Patel, V.V.: A new 3-dimensional method for measuring precision in surgical navigation and methods to optimize navigation accuracy. Eur. Spine J. **25**(6), 1764–1774 (2016)

7. Gstoettner, M., Lechner, R., Glodny, B., Thaler, M., Bach, C.M.: Inter- and intraobserver reliability assessment of computed tomographic 3D measurement of pedicles in scoliosis and size matching with pedicle screws. Eur. Spine J. **20**(10), 1771–1779 (2011)

8. Knez, D., Likar, B., Pernuš, F., Vrtovec, T.: Computer-assisted screw size and insertion trajectory planning for pedicle screw placement surgery. IEEE Trans. Med. Imaging **35**(6), 1420–1430 (2016)

9. Lee, J., Kim, S., Kim, Y.S., Chung, W.K.: Optimal surgical planning guidance for lumbar spinal fusion considering operational safety and vertebra-screw interface strength: optimal surgical planning guidance for lumbar spinal fusion. Int. J. Med. Robot. **8**(3), 261–272 (2012)

10. Schreiber, J.J.: Hounsfield units for assessing bone mineral density and strength: a tool for osteoporosis management. J. Bone Jt. Surg. Am. **93**(11), 1057–1063 (2011)

11. Linte, C.A., Augustine, K.E., Camp, J.J., Robb, R.A., Holmes III, D.R.: Toward virtual modeling and templating for enhanced spine surgery planning. In: Li, S., Yao, J. (eds.) Spinal Imaging and Image Analysis. LNCVB, vol. 18, pp. 441–467. Springer, Cham (2015)

12. Chapman, J.R., Harrington, R.M., Lee, K.M., Anderson, P.A., Tencer, A.F., Kowalski, D.: Factors affecting the pullout strength of cancellous bone screws. J. Biomech. Eng. **118**(3), 391–398 (1996)

13. Bianco, R.J., Arnoux, P.J., Wagnac, E., Mac-Thiong, J.M., Aubin, C.É.: Minimizing pedicle screw pullout risks: a detailed biomechanical analysis of screw design and placement. J. Spinal Disord. Tech. (2014). Publish Ahead of Print https://www.ncbi.nlm.nih.gov/pubmed/25075993

14. Hirano, T., Hasegawa, K., Takahashi, H.E., Uchiyama, S., Hara, T., Washio, T., Sugiura, T., Yokaichiya, M., Ikeda, M.: Structural characteristics of the pedicle and its role in screw stability. Spine **22**(21), 2504–2509 (1997)
15. Weinstein, J.N., Rydevik, B.L., Rauschning, W.: Anatomic and technical considerations of pedicle screw fixation. Clin. Orthop. **284**, 34–46 (1992)
16. Roy-Camille, R., Saillant, G., Mazel, C.: Internal fixation of the lumbar spine with pedicle screw plating. Clin. Orthop. **203**, 7–17 (1986)

Detection of Degenerative Osteophytes of the Spine on PET/CT Using Region-Based Convolutional Neural Networks

Yinong Wang[1], Jianhua Yao[1(✉)], Joseph E. Burns[2],
Jiamin Liu[1], and Ronald M. Summers[1]

[1] Imaging Biomarkers and Computer-Aided Diagnosis Laboratory,
Radiology and Imaging Sciences, Clinical Center, National Institutes of Health,
Bethesda, MD 20892, USA
jyao@cc.nih.gov
[2] Department of Radiological Sciences, University of California,
Irvine School of Medicine, Orange, CA 92868, USA

Abstract. The identification and detection of degenerative osteophytes of the spine is a challenging and time-consuming task that is important for the diagnosis of many spine diseases. Previous attempts to automate this task have been focused on using image features derived from radiographic diagnostic expertise rather than directly learning features. In this paper, we present a bottom-up approach to generate features for classification using a region-based convolutional neural network with unwrapped cortical shell maps from ^{18}F-NaF positron emission tomography and computed tomography scans of the vertebral bodies of the thoracic and lumbar spine. We evaluated osteophyte detection performance on 45 individuals with 5-fold cross validation and achieved state-of-the-art performance with 85% sensitivity at 2 false positive detections per patient.

Keywords: Osteophyte detection · Convolutional neural networks · ^{18}F-NaF PET/CT · Spine

1 Introduction

Osteophytes are bony outgrowths that develop along the margins of joints and disc spaces and have been linked to chronic and intense pain. Osteophytes of the spine become more prevalent with age, and are found in over 90% of the population age 60 years and above [8]. Further examinations show that osteophytes occur more often in men rather than women and in individuals whose occupations require regular heavy physical labor [9].

The identification and annotation of these pathologies on diagnostic imaging studies can be both time consuming and difficult to complete. However,

---

The rights of this work are transferred to the extent transferable according to title 17 §105 U.S.C.

© Springer International Publishing AG 2016 (outside the US)
J. Yao et al. (Eds.): CSI 2016, LNCS 10182, pp. 116–124, 2016.
DOI: 10.1007/978-3-319-55050-3_11

there have been increasing efforts to use computer-aided detection for identifying pathology of the spine and to segment these abnormal structures. By applying a series of successive level sets to segment the vertebra and to capture the curvature of both the endplates and the rim of the cortical shell, Tan et al. provided a technique to segment syndesmophytes, a similar type of bony outgrowth at the intervertebral disc (IVD) margins seen in individuals with ankylosing spondylitis [10]. Brown et al. developed a system using region-specific intensity thresholding on bone scans for identifying and segmenting metastatic lesions of the bone [3]. Additionally, on sodium fluoride (^{18}F-NaF) positron emission tomography (PET) and computed tomography (CT) studies, spinal osteophytes and sclerotic metastatic lesions can appear similar, creating false positive lesion detections and potentially altering therapy [2]. The development of these computer-aided detection algorithms provides a means to differentiate similar-looking pathology and to more comprehensively evaluate the spine for subsequent medical intervention.

In recent years, the use of deep learning (DL) and convolutional neural networks (CNNs) in medical image analysis has gained momentum and begun to replace the need for entire systems to be designed for specific problems as well as the difficult task of manually engineering distinct but robust features using prior understanding of the data. By learning features from the data and training the system in an end-to-end supervised manner, CNNs have outperformed more traditional machine learning methods by a significant margin on natural images [6]. More recent applications to medical imaging include the work of Bar et al., which showed that CNNs can improve the detection of pathology on chest x-rays over GIST descriptors, low dimensional feature vectors, as well as Bag-of-Visual-Words, a visual word dictionary [1]. Liu et al. applied region-based convolutional neural networks (R-CNN), an extensively tested visual object detection system, to the task of colitis detection in the colon and achieved performance nearing a threshold of acceptance for clinical use [7]. These results provide evidence that suggests the potential increase in detection performance by using CNNs is not limited to natural images.

Despite variability in shape, density, and location, radiologists generally identify spinal osteophytes on CT by their relatively high intensity and morphological projections at the IVD space margin, typically spanning multiple vertebra levels (Fig. 1). We revisit this task by utilizing previous efforts to detect osteophytes where Yao et al. used unwrapped surface representations of the cortical shell of vertebral bodies derived from ^{18}F-NaF PET/CT scans [12] with a three-tier classification scheme using region covariance matrices to detect spinal degenerative osteophytes [13]. We propose the application of a deep learning framework using R-CNN for feature acquisition [4], which leverages high-capacity convolutional neural networks with bottom-up region proposals, to unwrapped cortical shell images for the detection of spinal degenerative osteophytes using linear support vector machines (SVM).

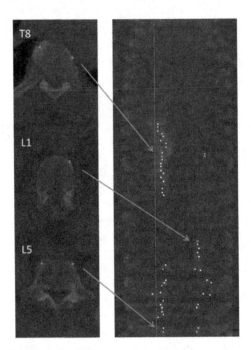

Fig. 1. Left: Axial view of annotated thoracic and lumbar vertebrae (T8, L1, L5) with spinal degenerative osteophytes (indicated by dots) on select CT slices and **Right:** corresponding unwrapped cortical shell feature map with selected annotations.

2   Methods

The method for detecting spinal degenerative osteophytes is outlined as follows (Fig. 2). Unwrapped cortical shell maps of the thoracic and lumbar vertebral bodies from PET/CT scans were assembled. After preprocessing the input images, region proposals were generated as inputs for feature learning by the CNN. Output feature vectors from the CNN were classified using a linear SVM. Detection boxes were then combined in order to evaluate osteophyte detection performance on a per-image basis.

2.1   Cortical Shell Unwrapping

Spinal degenerative osteophytes can be modeled on CT as high intensity protrusions of the cortex that project radially from the vertebral body. Understanding this fundamental component of where in the vertebrae they develop, the detection problem can be simplified. Rather than directly applying deep learning to entire PET/CT scans, unwrapped representations of the cortical shell of the vertebral bodies were produced [12]. This required the extraction of the spinal column and partitioning of all thoracic and lumbar vertebrae as described by Yao et al. [14].

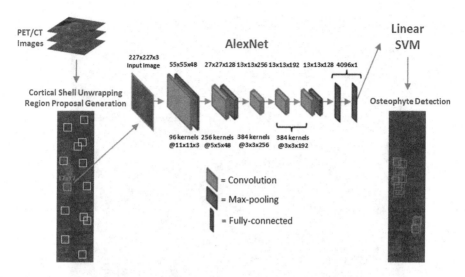

Fig. 2. Pipeline for spinal degenerative osteophyte detection. PET/CT scans used to create unwrapped cortical shell maps. Region proposals of patch size 17×17 were generated from the unwrapped maps, combined into a 3-channel RGB image, and upscaled to 227×227×3 inputs into the CNN. After propagating through the 5 convolutional, 3 max-pooling, and 2 fully-connected layers, a 4096-dimensional feature vector was used for classification via linear SVM and detection on full unwrapped map (ground truth in green, true positive detections in yellow, and false positive detections in red). (Color figure online)

By creating a deformable dual-surface model, both the endosteal and periosteal surfaces of the cortical shell were extracted using anatomical information from CT, producing a complete segmentation of the cortical layer. Because osteophytes appear as high intensity objects, they were captured by the cortical shell segmentation. The cortical shell volumes of each vertebra were then individually unwrapped by mapping into 2D space using cylindrical coordinates and realigned to form unwrapped maps of the full spine as seen in Fig. 1. This technique was identically applied to both CT and PET scans, and generated a series of feature maps of the cortical shell thickness, radius from the center of the vertebral body, and intensities on CT as well as standard uptake values (SUV) on PET shown in Fig. 3.

2.2   Region Proposal Generation

The region-based convolutional neural network learns features from bottom-up region proposals derived from the input images [4]. Although the original R-CNN package utilized selective search [11] as a means to generate category-independent region proposals by combining a graph-based segmentation method with a hierarchical grouping algorithm, we chose a fixed-size sliding window approach which was found to achieve significantly higher detection rates.

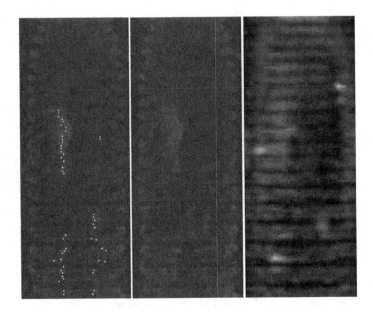

Fig. 3. Example unwrapped cortical shell images of the full spine with **Left:** annotated osteophytes (marked by white dots) on CT, **Middle:** cortical shell intensity on CT, and **Right:** cortical shell SUV on PET.

Experiments with region proposal size showed that patches of 17×17 pixels resulted in peak detection performance with an average of 20,000 region proposals per image.

2.3 CNN Network Architecture

The GPU-accelerated CUDA-based Caffe implementation [5] of the AlexNet CNN architecture by Krizhevsky et al. was used for the task of feature extraction [6]. The AlexNet architecture consists of 7 hidden layers, 5 convolutional layers, 3 max-pooling layers, and 2 fully-connected layers to produce a 4096-dimensional vector of features. One requirement of AlexNet is the use of 3-channel RGB image inputs. By reading separate maps from the CT and PET data as individual channels to formulate an RGB image, the CNN can utilize information from multiple imaging modalities in order to determine features for extraction. The network converted all 17×17 patch region proposals into a fixed size 227×227 patch 3-channel input image required by AlexNet.

2.4 CNN Training

In the case of performing an object detection task on small image datasets, it can be difficult to create a robust model by training a CNN from the ground up without over-fitting the classification results. However, by leveraging models built from existing datasets of natural images as large as hundreds of thousands of images, transfer learning provides a means to apply previously trained networks to a novel task such as spinal degenerative osteophyte detection. Network parameters can then be fine-tuned to our image domain in the later layers of the CNN while retaining the more generic image features learned from the pre-trained network.

The CNN was pre-trained on the ILSVRC2012 dataset[1], a widely-used dataset for benchmarking object detection algorithms. Domain-specific fine tuning was completed on the fully-connected layers using a subset of labeled training images after 50,000 iterations. The training of the network was completed by treating region proposals with ≥ 0.5 intersection over union (IoU) overlap with a given ground-truth box as a positive training example and ≤ 0.3 as negative examples. The rest of our method followed the original parameters described by Girshick et al., using stochastic gradient descent for optimizing the network parameters at a learning rate of 0.001 and linear SVM for the classification task [4]. Training was evaluated using the detection performance on a small subset of the training set and completed after 14 h on an 8-core Intel Xeon PC with a Nvidia GTX Titan Z GPU.

2.5 CNN Feature Extraction and SVM Classification

Features for classification were extracted as 4096-dimensional feature vectors for each region proposal. After acquiring feature vectors for all region proposals, a committee of linear support vector machines was used for the binary task of classifying spinal degenerative osteophytes [4]. A greedy non-maximum suppression algorithm was applied in order to reduce the number of overlapping detection boxes by selecting detections with a largest IoU with the ground-truth boxes. Detection boxes belonging to the same patient were aggregated in order to determine performance on a per-patient level.

3   Experiments and Results

3.1   Dataset

The dataset of 45 ^{18}F-NaF PET/CT scans used in this experiment was obtained with IRB approval. Scans were acquired on a Philips GEMINI TF scanner from 45 patients with anonymized demographics ranging from around 51 to 85 years old. Patients were intravenously administered a dose of ^{18}F-NaF ranging from 112×10^6–203×10^6 Bq/ml with a physiological uptake period of 114 to 126 min prior to PET image acquisition. Axial PET images of size 144×144 or 169×169 pixels were obtained with an axial spatial resolution of 4 mm$\times$4 mm per pixel and 4 mm slice spacing. CT images were obtained using a low dose technique with a 5 mm slice thickness, 120 kVp, no intravenous contrast, and convolution kernel B. Osteophytes were annotated by a trained radiologist on the axial CT slices, and osteophytes spanning multiple vertebra levels were condensed into one rectangular ground-truth box for CNN training and testing.

---

[1] http://image-net.org/.

3.2 Results

Performance was evaluated using free-response operating characteristic (FROC) curve analysis with 5-fold cross validation. All 3-channel images contained the cortical shell CT intensity and the cortical shell PET SUV maps as two of the three input channels. The addition of the trabecular CT intensity and the vertebral body radius maps as the third channel were compared. If the area of the detection box had ≥ 0.7 IoU with any ground-truth box, it was treated as a true positive detection and the remainder were treated as negatives. The threshold for true positive detection was based on a more selective value than the IoU threshold for CNN positive training sample selection (area ≥ 0.5 IoU) asince the lower training threshold was used to enforce greater variability for feature learning.

Using a combination of the cortical shell CT intensity and the cortical shell PET SUV with sliding window region proposals, a sensitivity of 85% at 2 false positives per patient (FPs/patient) and F1 score of 0.91 was achieved (Fig. 4). This effectively reduced the false positive rate by nearly 50% compared to the method of using handcrafted features from unwrapped cortical shell maps in Yao et al., which had a sensitivity of 84% at 3.8 FPs/patient [13]. In addition, at the same false positive rate of 3.8 FPs/patient, our method obtained a much higher

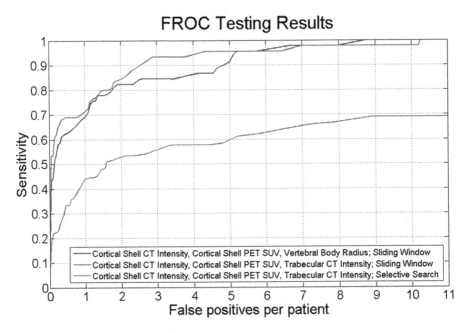

Fig. 4. Free-response operating characteristic (FROC) curves with 5-fold cross validation. The first two image channels fixed on cortical shell CT intensity and cortical shell PET SUV. Three configurations were compared: vertebral body radius as last channel with sliding window (blue), trabecular CT intensity with sliding window (red), and trabecular CT intensity with selective search (yellow). (Color figure online)

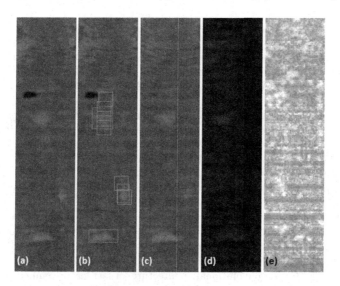

Fig. 5. Spinal osteophyte detection examples: **(a)** cortical shell CT intensity map, **(b)** cortical shell CT intensity map with detections: ground truth (green), true positive detections (yellow), and false positive detections (red), **(c)** trabecular CT intensity, **(d)** cortical shell PET SUV map, and **(e)** vertebral body radius map. (Color figure online)

sensitivity of 94%. Using sliding window for region proposal generation vastly outperformed selective search (F1 score of 0.69) which operated at a sensitivity of 53% at 2 FPs/patient (p-value $< 10^{-3}$), and the use of the vertebral body radius map (F1 score of 0.89) with a sensitivity of 82% at 2 FPs/patient did not produce any statistically significant performance benefits (p-value $= 0.527$). Examples of osteophyte detection results are shown in Fig. 5.

4 Conclusion

By following a previous method developed by Yao et al., our results can be evaluated as a more direct comparison of using learned features through R-CNN rather than hand-crafted features, and show a significant reduction in the amount of false positives generated on a per-patient level as well as a much higher sensitivity at a similar false positive rate [13]. In addition, with 45 patients, our dataset was more than twice the size of that used in the previous paper. These significant improvements in osteophyte detection may drive future investigative efforts to differentiate similarly appearing pathologies of the spine and interventional medical treatments.

Acknowledgments. This research was supported in part by the Intramural Research Program of National Institutes of Health Clinical Center.

References

1. Bar, Y., Diamant, I., Wolf, L., Lieberman, S., Konen, E., Greenspan, H.: Chest pathology detection using deep learning with non-medical training. In: IEEE 12th International Symposium on Biomedical Imaging (ISBI), 2015, pp. 294–297. IEEE (2015)
2. Bastawrous, S., Bhargava, P., Behnia, F., Djang, D.S., Haseley, D.R.: Newer pet application with an old tracer: role of 18F-NaF skeletal PET/CT in oncologic practice. Radiographics **34**(5), 1295–1316 (2014)
3. Brown, M.S., Chu, G.H., Kim, H.J., Allen-Auerbach, M., Poon, C., Bridges, J., Vidovic, A., Ramakrishna, B., Ho, J., Morris, M.J., et al.: Computer-aided quantitative bone scan assessment of prostate cancer treatment response. Nuclear Med. Commun. **33**(4), 384 (2012)
4. Girshick, R., Donahue, J., Darrell, T., Malik, J.: Rich feature hierarchies for accurate object detection and semantic segmentation. In: Proceedings of the IEEE Conference on Computer Vision and Pattern Recognition, pp. 580–587 (2014)
5. Jia, Y., Shelhamer, E., Donahue, J., Karayev, S., Long, J., Girshick, R., Guadarrama, S., Darrell, T.: Caffe: convolutional architecture for fast feature embedding. In: Proceedings of the ACM International Conference on Multimedia, pp. 675–678. ACM (2014)
6. Krizhevsky, A., Sutskever, I., Hinton, G.E.: Imagenet classification with deep convolutional neural networks. In: Advances in Neural Information Processing Systems, pp. 1097–1105 (2012)
7. Liu, J., Lay, N., Wei, Z., Lu, L., Kim, L., Turkbey, E., Summers, R.M.: Colitis detection on abdominal CT scans by rich feature hierarchies. In: SPIE Medical Imaging, p. 97851N. International Society for Optics and Photonics (2016)
8. Nathan, H.: Osteophytes of the vertebral column. J. Bone Joint Surg. Am. **44**(2), 243–268 (1962)
9. Resnick, D.: Degenerative diseases of the vertebral column. Radiology **156**(1), 3–14 (1985)
10. Tan, S., Yao, J., Ward, M.M., Yao, L., Summers, R.M.: Computer aided evaluation of ankylosing spondylitis. In: 3rd IEEE International Symposium on Biomedical Imaging: Nano to Macro, pp. 339–342. IEEE (2006)
11. Uijlings, J.R., van de Sande, K.E., Gevers, T., Smeulders, A.W.: Selective search for object recognition. Int. J. Comput. Vis. **104**(2), 154–171 (2013)
12. Yao, J., Burns, J.E., Munoz, H., Summers, R.M.: Detection of vertebral body fractures based on cortical shell unwrapping. In: Ayache, N., Delingette, H., Golland, P., Mori, K. (eds.) MICCAI 2012. LNCS, vol. 7512, pp. 509–516. Springer, Heidelberg (2012). doi:10.1007/978-3-642-33454-2_63
13. Yao, J., Munoz, H., Burns, J.E., Lu, L., Summers, R.M.: Computer aided detection of spinal degenerative osteophytes on Sodium Fluoride PET/CT. In: Yao, J., Klinder, T., Li, S. (eds.) Computational Methods and Clinical Applications for Spine Imaging. LNCVB, vol. 17, pp. 51–60. Springer, Cham (2014). doi:10.1007/978-3-319-07269-2_5
14. Yao, J., O'Connor, S.D., Summers, R.M.: Automated spinal column extraction and partitioning. In: 3rd IEEE International Symposium on Biomedical Imaging: Nano to Macro, pp. 390–393. IEEE (2006)

Reconstruction of 3D Lumvar Vertebra from Two X-ray Images Based on 2D/3D Registration

Longwei Fang[1,2], Zuowei Wang[4,5], Zhiqiang Chen[1,2],
Fengzeng Jian[4], and Huiguang He[1,2,3(✉)]

[1] Research Center for Brain-inspired Intelligence, Institute of Automation,
Chinese Academy of Sciences, Beijing, China
huiguang.he@ia.ac.cn
[2] University of Chinese Academy of Sciences, Beijing, China
[3] Center for Excellence in Brain Science and Intelligence Technology,
Chinese Academy of Sciences, Beijing, China
[4] Division of Spine, Department of Neurosurgery, Xuanwu Hospital, China
International Neurological Institute, Capital Medical University, Beijing, China
[5] Department of Neurosurgery, Beijing Hospital, Beijing, China

Abstract. Constructing a 3D bone from two X-ray images is a challenging task, especially when we would like to build a complicated structure like spine. This paper presents a novel method for reconstructing lumbar vertebra by building correspondence of two X-ray images with a prior model. First, the pose between X-ray images and the vertebra model was estimated; second, the correspondences between the Digitally Reconstructed Radiographies (DRRs) and vertebra model were built; third, the deformation field from DRRs to X-ray images was calculated; last, deformation field was applied to vertebra model to generate the patient's specified 3D model. This method just needs one prior model for 3D reconstruction. The experiments on nine vertebrae of three patients show the average reconstruction error is 1.2 mm (1.0 mm–1.3 mm) which is comparable to the state of the art.

Keywords: 3D reconstruction · Lumbar vertebra model · X-ray images · 2D/3D registration · 2D/2D deformable registration

1 Introduction

Image-guided radiotherapy has been more and more widely used in the hospital. Images shown in 3D form are very useful and convenient for the doctor to understand the pathology. Generally, the Computed Tomography (CT) or Magnetic Resonance Image (MRI) is used to reconstruct the patient's 3D model, however, it is difficult and inconvenient to collect CT/MRI data in operation. Therefore, the technique that use X-ray images to construct patient's 3D model is developed recently [1–7].

© Springer International Publishing AG 2016
J. Yao et al. (Eds.): CSI 2016, LNCS 10182, pp. 125–134, 2016.
DOI: 10.1007/978-3-319-55050-3_12

Statistical Shape Model (SSM) or Point Distribution Model (PDM) was widely used [1–4] for 3D reconstruction. Zheng et al. [5] used two X-ray images and a PDM to construct distal femur. Contours of the surface defined by the PDM were projected into two 2D planes and established correspondences with features detected from fluoroscopic images; these contour points were then back-projected into 3D space, reconstructed into 3D points; then those points were registered to the corresponding 3D point set by deforming the point distribution model to generate patient specified model. Prakoonwit et al. [6] reconstructed distal femur using several X-ray images and a SSM by camera calibration technique. The correspondences between X-ray images were built by camera calibration, and then the correspondence points was back-projected into 3D space and reconstructed into 3D point set, then the statistical shape model was deformed by registering to those points. Whitmarsh et al. [3] proposes a method that using statistical shape model combined with statistical density model to reconstruct patient lumbar vertebrae model. In prepare phase, statistical shape model and statistical density model was constructed from a large dataset of QCT scans, in reconstruction phase, the models were simultaneously registered onto the two DXA images by an intensity based 2D/3D registration process, then the optimized registration was found by adjust the parameters of statistical model. This optimized registration model is the reconstructed patient specified model.

There are some deficiencies in existing methods. Only the boundary or profile of the X-ray images were used [1,2,4–6] to restrict the deformation of the SSM or PDM, they do not make good use of the intensity information inside the boundary. Other methods [3,7] use the intensity information of the whole 2D X-ray images, but the construction speed is very slow as they need to calculate the probability distribution of the shape model in each iteration.

The nature of SSM/PDM method is using a large number of collecting data to build a mean model and a set of deformable parameters, then giving those deformable parameters different weights and adding them to mean shape to generate a series of model and choose one that has the minimal difference with specific patient model. Therefore, the accuracy of those reconstruction methods depend heavily on the unknown patient-specific shape variation covered by the SSM/PDM [8]. In real clinic cases, the pathology spine maybe have a strange shape, the SSM or PDM unable to cover an arbitrary pathology. Actually, if we can find a way to calculate the difference between the prior model and the real data, then we can generate the specific patient model by deforming the prior model with those difference, this kind of method do not rely on the coverage of model shape and can handle more complex cases.

In this paper, we propose a novel methods that using two X-ray images and a prior vertebral model to reconstruct the patient specified vertebral. We only use one vertebral model as prior knowledge, all the deformation are completed in 2D images, the 3D reconstruction accuracy is comparable to the state of art, and the reconstruction speed is fast.

This paper is organized as follows. Section 2 presents the details of reconstruction procedure. Section 3 describes the experiment design and the result, the discussion and conclusion is in Sect. 4.

2   Meterials and Methods

2.1   Brief Introduction of Reconstruction

The main idea is that we introduce a prior model into our method, and we estimate the pose, position and the deformation between the X-ray images and the
prior model, and then we apply these parameters to deform the prior model to
get the final 3D specific patient model. The whole reconstruction process was
divided into four parts: First, the pose between X-ray images and the vertebral
model was estimated; second, the correspondence between DRRs and vertebral
model was built; third, the deformation field from DRRs to X-ray images was
calculated; last, deformation field was applied to the vertebra model to generate the patient specified 3D model. Figure 1 is the flow diagram of the whole
reconstruction process.

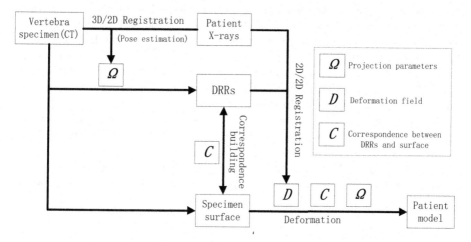

Fig. 1. The flow diagram of the whole reconstruction process

2.2   Data Collection

The CT data of vertebra model or prior model was provided by Beijing
Hospital, the model is the third lumbar vertebrae in human body. The
data collecting device is GE Discovery HD720, and the resolution of CT is
$0.24\,\text{mm} * 0.24\,\text{mm} * 0.7\,\text{mm}$. The vertebra specimen is labelled with thirteen
landmarks before data collection, six landmarks were posted on vertebra body,
one was on spinous process, two were on transverse process and two were on the
superior articular process. Figure 2(a) shows the picture of landmarks on vertebra model and Fig. 2(b) is the reconstructed 3D CT image of vertebra model.

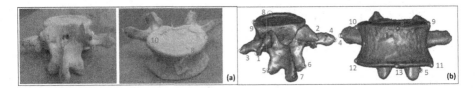

Fig. 2. Landmarks position on vertebra model (a) Landmarks on physical model (b) landmarks on reconstructed CT images

2.3   Pose Estimation Between X-ray Images and Vertebra Model

The projection parameters are the position and pose of the two ray sources when combining the X-ray images and the lumbar vertebra CT into the same coordinate. Two steps were needed to estimate the projection parameters: the reconstructed lumbar vertebrae was segmented from X-ray images and the landmarks were labelled on the segmented images; and the landmarks based 2D/3D rigid registration between X-ray images and the vertebra model. Figure 3(a) shows the calculation procedure of projection parameters. We used the Intelligent Scissors [9] to segment the vertebra. After segmentation, landmarks should be labeled on the segmented image according to the markers position on vertebra model shown in Fig. 2(a). We just labeled the landmarks that can be seen on the segmented image, the landmarks labeled in two images can be different.

We assumed that the distance of the CT center to projection plane is fixed. V_{pc}^i, V_{ps}^i represent the projection of landmarks on coronal and sagittal plane, separately; V_{xc}^i, V_{xs}^i represent the landmarks of X-ray images on coronal and sagittal plane, separately. We assumed that the distance of the ray source to projection plane is d, then we can use Eq. 1 to solve the projection parameters.

$$\Omega = \underset{\Omega=(\Omega_1,\Omega_2)}{\arg\max} \left(\sum_i^M \|V_{pc}^i(\Omega_1) - V_{xc}^i\|^2 + \sum_j^N \|V_{ps}^j(\Omega_2) - V_{xs}^j\|^2 \right) \qquad (1)$$

In Eq. (1), the origin of coordinate system is the center of CT data, $\| \cdot \|$ is the Euclidean distance; $\Omega_1 = \{r_{x1}, r_{y1}, r_{z1}, t_{x1}, t_{z1}\}$, $\Omega_1 = \{r_{x2}, r_{y2}, r_{z2}, t_{x2}, t_{z2}\}$ is the projection parameters of two ray source; r_{x*}, r_{y*}, r_{z*} is the rotate angle along three axis, t_{x*}, t_{z*} is the translation along x and z axis; M represents the landmarks on coronal plane, N represents the landmarks on sagittal plane.

2.4   Building Correspondence Between Projection Images and Vertebra Model

This process could be achieved by three steps: vertebra model surface extraction, DRRs generation, projecting control points into DRRs. Figure 3(b) shows the correspondence building between projection images and vertebra model.

First, the surface of the lumbar vertebra model was extracted. The vertexes of the mesh were the control points which were used to reconstruct the patient specified vertebra model. The number of the vertices was 3500.

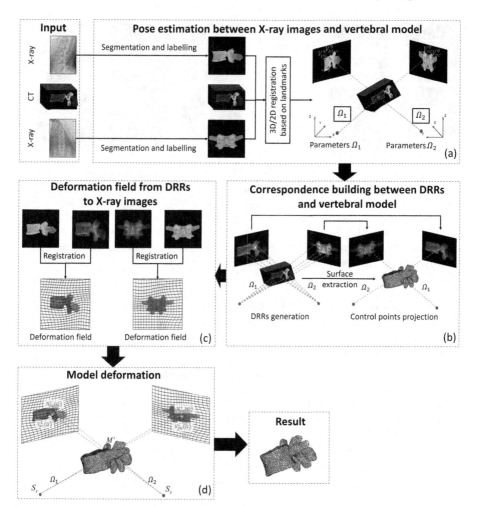

Fig. 3. The flow chart of whole reconstruction process (a) shows the pose estimation between X-ray images and vertebra model (b) shows the correspondence built between DRRs and vertebra model (c) shows the flow chart of calculating deformation field (d) shows the process of model deformation to generate the specific patient model

Second, projection images or DRRs were generated by projecting the CT data into projection planes. We used the ray casting algorithm [10] to generate the DRRs. Figure 4(a) shows the DRRs in coronal and sagittal plane, separately.

Last, the intersection coordinates that lines which are Connect the ray source and control points with projection planes (DRRs plane) were calculated. Dividing the intersection coordinates by the pixel space and rounding the result, we will find the correspondence location on the DRRs for the projection of the control points. The projection of the same control point in two planes are a control point pair and the projection of control points moved when the correspondence

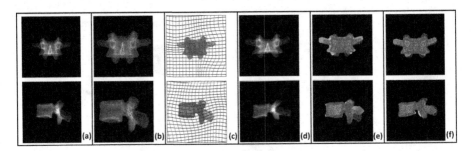

Fig. 4. The intermediate result of calculating deformation field of projection images (a) DRRs generated from CT data (b) projection of control points (c) deformation field after deformable registration, we change the background into white for clearly showing the deformation field (d) results of deformation on DRRs (e) projection of control points mapping in X-ray images before registration (f) projection of control points mapping in X-ray images after registration. The red dots in above images are the projection of same control point (Color figure online)

pixels in DRRs moved. Figure 4(b) shows the projection of the control points in the coronal and sagittal plane separately, the reds ones are the projection of a same control point.

2.5 Calculating the Deformation Field from DRRs to X-ray Images

The deformation field from DRRs to X-ray images was calculated by Free-Form Deformation registration method [11]. Figure 3(c) shows the flow chart of calculation. Figure 4(c) is the deformation field after registration, Fig. 4(d) is the deformation result of DRRs, Fig. 4(e) is the projection of control points mapping into the X-ray images before registration and Fig. 4(f) is the projection of control points mapping in the X-ray images after registration.

2.6 Model Deformation

We assume $V_{pc}^i(\Omega)$, $V_{ps}^i(\Omega)$ are the projection of the same control point in coronal and sagittal plane separately, where $V_{pc}^i(\Omega) = [x_c^i, y_c^i]^T$, $V_{ps}^i(\Omega) = [x_s^i, y_s^i]^T$; D_{pc}^i, D_{ps}^i represent deformation vector in coronal projection image and sagittal projection image separately, where $D_{pc}^i = [d_{cx}^i, d_{cy}^i]^T$, $D_{ps}^i = [d_{sx}^i, d_{sy}^i]^T$; and $[d_{*x}, d_{*y}]^T$ is the deformation in position $[x, y]^T$. N_{pc}^i, N_{ps}^i are the new position of control point's projection after deformation in two planes. Then we have

$$\begin{cases} N_{pc}^i = V_{pc}^i(\Omega) + D_{pc}^i = [x_c^i + d_{cx}^i, y_c^i + d_{cy}^i]^T \\ N_{ps}^i = V_{ps}^i(\Omega) + D_{ps}^i = [x_s^i + d_{sx}^i, y_s^i + d_{sy}^i]^T \end{cases} \tag{2}$$

The intersection point M^i by the line $S_c N_{pc}^i(\Omega)$ and line $S_s N_{ps}^i(\Omega)$ is the new position of the control point i. Figure 3(d) shows the deformation of vertebra model.

3   Experiments and Results

3.1   Experiments Design

The X-ray images of three patients were used to validate the method, and the X-ray images were shown in Fig. 5. L2, L3 and L4 of the lumbar vertebra were chose for reconstruction. We segmented vertebra model from corresponding CT and extracted its surface as the ground truth, the vertex number of the surface was 3500. The average distance from reconstructed mesh to the ground truth was regard as reconstruction error. For the experiment, we used 18 Inter(R) Xeon(R) CPU e5-2687w @3.10 GHz with 64 G RAM, the operation system is CentOS6.3 and the programming language is C++ mixed with MATLAB.

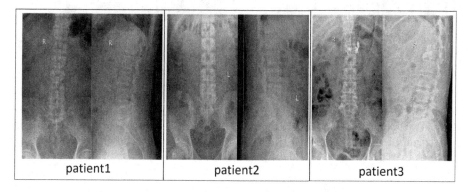

Fig. 5. The X-ray images of three patients

3.2   Result

We used the proposed method to reconstruct L2, L3 and L4 lumbar vertebra successfully, the average reconstruction error was 1.2 mm (1.0 mm–1.3 mm), and the average reconstruction time was 45 s. Table 1 shows the reconstruction error and time of each lumbar vertebra, and Fig. 6 shows the result of reconstruction, for each patient, the left column is the ground truth with the color-coded error distribution; the middle column shows the result of reconstruction; right column is the histogram of the reconstruction error, 95% of the reconstruction error less than the value in red line.

Table 1. Reconstruction error and time of all three patients

Case	P1-L2	P1-L3	P1-L4	P2-L2	P2-L3	P2-L4	P3-L2	P3-L3	P3 -L4
Error (mm)	1.2 ± 1.1	1.3 ± 1.3	1.3 ± 1.0	1.2 ± 1.0	1.2 ± 1.0	1.3 ± 1.2	1.1 ± 0.8	1.0 ± 0.8	1.2 ± 1.0
Time (s)	46	42	43	48	44	45	45	47	44

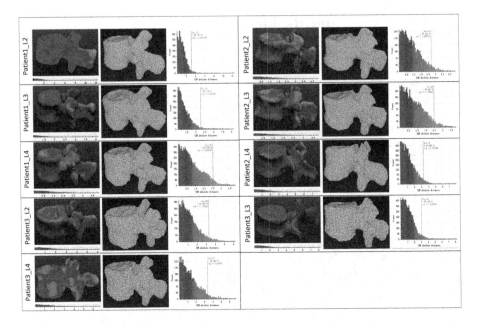

Fig. 6. Reconstruction result. For each patient, left column is ground truth models with the color-coded error distributions; middle column is the reconstruction result, right column is the histogram of the reconstruction error, 95% of the reconstruction error less than the value in red line (Color figure online)

4   Discussion and Conclusion

We proposed a novel method to reconstruct lumbar vertebra with two X-ray images and showed its application on nine lumbar vertebras. This novel method performed reconstruction by building correspondence of two X-ray images with a known lumbar vertebra model, it was tested in nine lumbar vertebras of three patients, the average reconstruction error was 1.2 mm (1.0 mm–1.3 mm) and the average construction time was 45 s. The experiments showed the good performance of our method in reconstruction.

The main difference between the present technique and the other works [1–7] lies in the fact that we use one prior model rather than SSM/PDM to reconstruct the specific patient model. We calculate the difference between the patient images and the prior knowledge and then add this difference to prior model to generate the specific patient model while the SSM/PDM based method build a series model and choose one that has a minimal difference with the patient date. What's more, we use the full information of the X-ray images rather than the boundary information of the information and the iteration process is finished in 2D images in our method, not in the 3D model, so the reconstruction speed is very fast. Moreover, the control points of our method evenly distribute in the whole ROI of the segmented X-ray images, as shown in Fig. 4(f), while the other methods [4–6] just distribute along the boundary of images.

There are some deficiencies in present approach. First, it needs to segment the reconstructed lumbar vertebra from X-ray image and add landmarks manually, although the reconstruction process does not take much time, the segmentation takes a lot of time; second, the reconstruction accuracy depends heavily on 2D/2D deformable registration between X-ray images and DRRs, the reconstruction error will be large when the registration result is not good. Nonetheless, the experiments from the present study demonstrate that this method will be more widely used in the future if it can cooperate with other auto segmentation methods and a more accurate 2D/2D registration method.

Acknowledgements. This work was supported by 863 Projects (2013AA013803), National Natural Science Foundation of China (61271151, 91520202) and Youth Innovation Promotion Association CAS.

References

1. Baka, N., Kaptein, B., de Bruijne, M., van Walsum, T., Giphart, J., Niessen, W.J., Lelieveldt, B.P.: 2D–3D shape reconstruction of the distal femur from stereo X-ray imaging using statistical shape models. Med. Image Anal. **15**(6), 840–850 (2011)
2. Humbert, L., De Guise, J., Aubert, B., Godbout, B., Skalli, W.: 3D reconstruction of the spine from biplanar X-rays using parametric models based on transversal and longitudinal inferences. Med. Eng. Phys. **31**(6), 681–687 (2009)
3. Whitmarsh, T., Humbert, L., Barquero, L.M.D.R., Di Gregorio, S., Frangi, A.F.: 3D reconstruction of the lumbar vertebrae from anteroposterior and lateral dual-energy X-ray absorptiometry. Med. Image Anal. **17**(4), 475–487 (2013)
4. Benameur, S., Mignotte, M., Labelle, H., De Guise, J.A.: A hierarchical statistical modeling approach for the unsupervised 3-D biplanar reconstruction of the scoliotic spine. IEEE Trans. Biomed. Eng. **52**(12), 2041–2057 (2005)
5. Zheng, G., Gollmer, S., Schumann, S., Dong, X., Feilkas, T., Ballester, M.A.G.: A 2D/3D correspondence building method for reconstruction of a patient-specific 3D bone surface model using point distribution models and calibrated X-ray images. Med. Image Anal. **13**(6), 883–899 (2009)
6. Prakoonwit, S.: Towards multiple 3D bone surface identification and reconstruction using few 2D X-ray images for intraoperative applications. Int. J. Art Cult. Des. Technol. **4**, 13–31 (2014)
7. Yao, J., Taylor, R.: Assessing accuracy factors in deformable 2D/3D medical image registration using a statistical pelvis model. In: 2003 Proceedings of the Ninth IEEE International Conference on Computer Vision, pp. 1329–1334. IEEE (2003)
8. Zheng, G., Nolte, L.-P.: Reconstruction of 3D vertebral models from a single 2D lateral fluoroscopic image. In: Li, S., Yao, J. (eds.) Spinal Imaging and Image Analysis. LNCVB, vol. 18, pp. 349–365. Springer, Cham (2015). doi:10.1007/978-3-319-12508-4_11
9. Mortensen, E.N., Barrett, W.A.: Intelligent scissors for image composition. In: Proceedings of the 22nd Annual Conference on Computer Graphics and Interactive Techniques, pp. 191–198. ACM (1995)

10. Jacobs, F., Sundermann, E., De Sutter, B., Christiaens, M., Lemahieu, I.: A fast algorithm to calculate the exact radiological path through a pixel or voxel space. CIT J. Comput. Inf. Technol. **6**(1), 89–94 (2015)
11. Mattes, D., Haynor, D.R., Vesselle, H., Lewellen, T.K., Eubank, W.: PET-CT image registration in the chest using free-form deformations. IEEE Trans. Med. Imaging **22**(1), 120–128 (2003)

Classification of Progressive and Non-progressive Scoliosis Patients Using Discriminant Manifolds

William Mandel[1], Robert Korez[1,2], Marie-Lyne Nault[2], Stefan Parent[2,3], and Samuel Kadoury[1,2(✉)]

[1] MedICAL, École Polytechnique de Montréal, Montréal, Canada
samuel.kadoury@polymtl.ca
[2] CHU Sainte-Justine Research Center, Montréal, Canada
[3] Department of Surgery, Université de Montréal, Montréal, Canada

Abstract. Adolescent idiopathic scoliosis (AIS) is a 3-D deformation of the spine. Identifying curve progression in AIS at the first visit is a clinically relevant problem but remains challenging due to lack of relevant descriptors. We present here a classification framework to identify patients whose spine deformity will progress from those who will remain stable. The method uses personalized 3-D spine reconstructions at baseline from progressive (P) and non-progressive (NP) patients to train a predictive model. Morphological changes between groups are detected using a manifold learning algorithm based on Grassmannian kernels in order to assess the similarity between shape topology and inter-vertebral poses in both groups (P, NP). We test the method to classify 52 progressive and 81 non-progressive patients enrolled in a prospective clinical study, yielding classification rates comparing favorably to standard classification methods.

1 Introduction

Adolescent idiopathic scoliosis (AIS) is a three-dimensional (3-D) deformation of the spine with unknown aetiopathogenesis. For children between 6 and 17 years old, the prevalence of AIS with a principal curvature greater than 10° is of 1.34%. A large scale study demonstrated that close to 40% of children screened at school and subsequently followed by a clinician are diagnosed with AIS [1]. One of the most challenging problems in AIS is the effective prediction of curve progression from a patient's baseline visit, once they are diagnosed with this pathology. In current clinical practice, factors such as patient maturity, including age and skeletal maturity using Risser sign, menarchal status, curve magnitude and curve location are used to assess a curve's probability for progression. These parameters are often used to establish treatment strategies, such as surgery or orthopedic braces, as well as scheduling follow-up examinations. Methods based

This study was Supported by NSERC, CHU Sainte-Justine Academic Research Chair in Spinal Deformities, the Canada Research Chair in Medical Imaging and Assisted Interventions.

J. Yao et al. (Eds.): CSI 2016, LNCS 10182, pp. 135–145, 2016.
DOI: 10.1007/978-3-319-55050-3_13

on alignment charts were made by [2] to link progression incidences with specific types of deformation, however these could not stratify progressive from non-progressive cases to determine optimal treatment strategies. Curve progression has become the primary concern for both patients and their families as it can cause significant distress from both an aesthetic and lifestyle perspective.

In recent years, spine morphology and in particular 3-D morphometric para-meters have shown significant promise to assess the link with respect to curve progression. In orthopaedics, 3-D spine models generated from medical images can assist specialists in the diagnosis of deformations and for the surgical plan-ning of patients, by providing an accurate modeling and landmark localization for deformed articulated spine segments. A retrospective evaluation of 3-D para-meters based on spinal and vertebral morphology was performed to classify pro-gressive and non-progressive patients [3]. More recently, a prospective study was performed to evaluate the differences in 3-D morphological spine parameters between both AIS groups using the patient's first visit [4]. These prediction sys-tems are derived from the clustering of hand-engineered parameters, which were calculated from 3-D spine reconstructions. However, relying on geometric indices sets out on a quest in search of the best characteristics to describe the 3-D nature of scoliotic spines.

Contrary to explicit parametric models, numerical or statistical methods are able to capture within a simplified space, the highly dimensional and complex nature of a fully geometric 3-D reconstruction of the spine, both on a regional (spinal) and local (vertebra) level. Ultimately, 3-D spine models could be inter-preted implicitly instead of using expert-based features which were examined in previous studies. While wavelet-based compression was used to assess spine curvature [5], manifold learning performed on locally linear embeddings was able to reduce the dimensionality of thoracic 3-D spine models [6]. Non-linear embeddings have been investigated in numerous studies based on probabilis-tic Gaussian [7] or spectral latent variables [8]. Indeed, they seek to preserve neighborhood relationships of similar object geometries, thereby revealing the underlying structure of the data which can be used for statistical modeling. Unfortunately, these dimensionality reduction algorithms based on local estima-tion are prone to the out of sample problem and sensitive to samples which map outside the normal distribution of the observed data. Recent studies based on deep learning algorithms such as stacked auto-encoders have successfully repre-sented multiple types of spinal deformations, but was limited to retrospective classification analysis [9].

The objective of this study is to propose a classifier which distinguishes between patients whose main curve will progress over 6° from those whose pro-gression is under 6° at follow-up. First, geometric spine models are reconstructed in 3-D from calibrated bi-planar radiographs to create a training set of person-alized scoliotic shapes. Once a training set of spine shapes is created for patients of these two clinically relevant groups (P, NP), a discriminant manifold based on Grassmannian kernels [10] is trained using the approach by [10] to maximize the separation between these two groups and improve the prediction accuracy for any unseen baseline reconstruction, which can be processed by mapping the 3-D spine model onto the trained manifold. The main contribution of this paper is to develop a prediction pipeline for curve progression based on their Grassmannian space representation. The paper is structured as follows. Section 2 presents the method in terms of geometric modeling and manifold training. Experiments are shown in Sect. 3, with a discussion in Sect. 4 and a conclusion in Sect. 5.

2   Methods

The input to our prediction approach is a collection of 3-D spine models which comprises a set of learning shapes with pose vectors for each level from progressive (P) and non-progressive (NP) AIS patients. These shapes are a constellation of annotated vertebrae with landmarks defined as characteristic points uniquely localized across a set of objects. We first build a discriminant manifold structure based on Grassmannian kernels from a training database to differentiate P and NP curves by embedding the data into a low-dimensional sub-space, the dimensionality of which corresponds to the domain of admissible variations.

2.1   3-D Spine Reconstruction from Sparse and Shape+Pose Modeling

In order to reconstruct the spine in 3-D, a coarse-to-fine modeling framework previously developed for the 3-D reconstruction of the scoliotic spine from biplanar X-ray images was used in this study [11]. First, the spine centerline, which is represented by the cubic spline in terms of its control points and local polynomial coefficients, is extracted from input biplanar radiographic images and used as a data descriptor for the underlying sparse modeling approach in order to obtain the initial 3-D reconstruction. By finding a sparse representation of the input descriptor, non-Gaussian errors (e.g. noisy and erroneous extracted centerlines) can be accounted for during the reconstruction process. We then adapt a multi-object pose+shape model proposed by Bossa and Olmos [12], where pose and shape variations are separately extracted and then correlated to present a joint pose+shape model. In contrast to articulated models, pose parameters were represented by similarity transformations, separately for each vertebral level. To obtain the final 3-D reconstruction of the scoliotic spine S, the pose+shape model is fitted to spine landmarks that were initially reconstructed by sparse modeling and later adjusted using a semi-automatic method to refine landmark positions [13].

To train the shape+pose model, a database consisting of 804 pairs of biplanar X-ray images of AIS patients was used. For each patient, a 3-D reconstruction of its spine (17 vertebrae in total) was generated from 3-D anatomical landmarks using the approach described above, and validated by an expert on digital radiographs. Six anatomical landmarks were identified on each vertebra from the first thoracic (T1) to the last lumbar (L5), i.e. two adjacent landmarks on superior and inferior vertebral endplates, and four landmarks at the tips of both pedicles.

Furthermore, each 3-D reconstruction was normalized against the spine height, i.e. the distance between the T1 center superior endplate landmark, denoted by l_{T1}, and the L5 center inferior endplate landmark, denoted by l_{L5}. A common (default) coordinate system for each 3-D reconstruction in the training database was established by applying the Gram-Schmidt orthonormalization procedure on a set of vectors $\{l_{T1} - l_{L5}, e_2, e_2 \times (l_{T1} - l_{L5})\}$, where $e_2 = [0, 1, 0]^T$. Finally, the matrix $R = [r_1, r_2, \dots, r_L] \in \mathbb{R}^{3M \times L}$ represented 3-D spine reconstructions stacked side-by-side, where each $r_i \in \mathbb{R}^{3M \times 1}$, $i = 1, 2, \dots, L$ vertebra levels, corresponded to the concatenation of 3-D coordinates of all $M = 6 \cdot 17$ ground truth landmarks from the i-th spine. The same six precise anatomical landmarks (4 pedicle tips and 2 on the vertebral body) were annotated on each triangulated model as shown in Fig. 1. The coordinates for each anatomical point were used to generate 3-D meshes for each vertebral body which defines the position and rotation (i.e. the ground-truth 3-D pose).

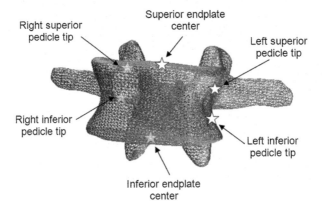

Fig. 1. Annotated landmarks on the triangulated mesh model of the first lumbar vertebra, with the 4 pedicle tips and 2 vertebral body centers.

2.2 Progression Prediction Using Discriminant Grassmannian Manifolds

Manifold learning algorithms are based on the premise that data are often of artificially high dimension and can be embedded in a lower dimensional space. However the presence of outliers and multi-class information can on the other hand affect the discrimination and/or generalization ability of the manifold. We propose to learn the optimal separation between two classes (1) non-progressive (NP) AIS patients and (2) progressive (P) AIS patients, by using a discriminant graph-embedding [10]. Each reconstructed spine model S can be viewed as the set of low-dimensional m subspaces of $\mathbb{R}^n$ on a Grassmannian manifold and represented by orthonormal matrices, each with a size of $n \times m$, with n the higher dimensionality of vertices defined earlier. Two points on a Grassmannian manifold are equivalent if one can be mapped into the other one by a $m \times m$ orthogonal matrix. In this work, similarity between two models (S_i, S_j) on the manifold is measured as a linear combination of projection and canonical correlation Grassmannian kernels $\mathbb{K}_{i,j}$ defined in the Hilbert Space by weighting parameters. By describing different features of the spine shape with each kernel, $\mathbb{K}_{i,j}$ can improve discriminatory accuracy between shapes.

In order to effectively discover the low-dimensional embedding, it is necessary to maintain the local structure of the data in the new embedding. The structure $G = (V, W)$ is an undirected similarity graph, with a collection of nodes V connected by edges, and the symmetric matrix W describing the edges between nodes of the graph. The diagonal matrix D and the Laplacian matrix L are defined as $L = D - W$, with $D(i,i) = \sum_{j \neq i} W_{ij} \forall i$. Here, N labelled spine models $\mathbb{S} = \{(S_i, c_i)\}_{i=1}^{N}$ are generated from the underlying manifold $\mathcal{M}$, where c_i denotes the label (NP or P). The task at hand is to maximize a measure of discriminatory power by mapping the underlying data into a vector space, while preserving similarities between data points in the high-dimensional space. Discriminant graph-embedding based on locally linear embedding (LLE) [14] uses graph-preserving criterions to maintain these similarities, which are included in a sparse and symmetric $N \times N$ matrix, denoted as M.

Within and between similarity graphs: In our work, the geometrical structure of $\mathcal{M}$ can be modeled by building a within-class similarity graph W_w for spine models of the same group and a between-class similarity graph W_b, to separate spine models from the two classes. When constructing the discriminant LLE graph, elements are partitioned into W_w and W_b classes. The intrinsic graph G is first created by assigning edges only to samples of the same class (e.g. NP). The local reconstruction coefficient matrix $M(i,j)$ is obtained by minimizing:

$$\min_{M} \sum_{j \in \mathcal{N}_w(i)} \|S_i - M(i,j)S_j\|^2 \quad \sum_{j \in \mathcal{N}_w(i)} M(i,j) = 1 \quad \forall i \qquad (1)$$

with $\mathcal{N}_w(i)$ as the neighborhood of size k_1, within the same region as point i (e.g. 3-D spine model from a NP patient). Each sample is therefore reconstructed only from 3-D model of the same clinical group. The local reconstruction coefficients are incorporated in the within-class similarity graph, such that the matrix W_w is defined as:

$$W_w(i,j) = \begin{cases} (M + M^T - M^T M)_{ij}, & \text{if } S_i \in \mathcal{N}_w(S_j) \text{ or } S_j \in \mathcal{N}_w(S_i) \\ 0, & \text{otherwise.} \end{cases} \qquad (2)$$

Conversely, the between-class similarity matrix W_b depicts the statistical properties to be avoided in the optimization process and used as a high-order constraint. Distances between P and NP samples are computed as:

$$W_b(i,j) = \begin{cases} 1/k_2, & \text{if } S_i \in \mathcal{N}_b(S_j) \text{ or } S_j \in \mathcal{N}_b(S_i) \\ 0, & \text{otherwise} \end{cases} \qquad (3)$$

with $\mathcal{N}_b$ containing k_2 neighbors having different class labels from the ith sample. The objective is to transform points to a new manifold $\mathcal{M}'$ of dimensionality d, i.e. $S_i \rightarrow y_i$, by mapping connected samples from the same group in $\boldsymbol{W}_w$ as close as possible to the class cluster, while moving P and NP models of $\boldsymbol{W}_b$ as far away from one another as possible. This results in optimizing the objective functions:

$$f_1 = \min_y \frac{1}{2} \sum_{i,j} (y_i - y_j)^2 \, \boldsymbol{W}_w(i,j) \quad f_2 = \max_y \frac{1}{2} \sum_{i,j} (y_i - y_j)^2 \, \boldsymbol{W}_b(i,j) \quad (4)$$

Supervised manifold learning: The optimal projection matrix, mapping new points to the manifold, is obtained by simultaneously maximizing class separability and preserving interclass manifold property, as described by the objective functions in Eq. (4). Assuming points on the manifold are known as similarity measures given by the Grassmannian kernel $\mathbb{K}_{i,j}$, a linear solution can be defined, i.e., $y_i = (\langle \alpha_1, S_i \rangle, \ldots, \langle \alpha_r, S_i \rangle)^T$ for the r largest eigenvectors with $\alpha_i = \sum_{j=1}^N a_{ij} S_j$. Defining the coefficient $\boldsymbol{A}_l = (a_{l1}, \ldots, a_{lN})^T$ and kernel $\boldsymbol{K}_i = (k_{i1}, \ldots, k_{iN})^T$ vectors, the output can be described as $y_i = \langle \alpha_l, S_i \rangle = \boldsymbol{A}_l^T \boldsymbol{K}_i$. By replacing the linear solution in the minimization and maximization of the between- and within-class graphs, the optimal projection matrix $\mathbb{A}$ is acquired from the optimization of the function as proposed in [10]. The proposed algorithm uses the points on the Grassmannian manifold implicitly (i.e., via measuring similarities through a kernel) to obtain a mapping $\mathbb{A}$. The matrix maximizes a quotient similar to discriminant analysis, while retaining the overall geometrical structure. Hence for any unseen 3-D spine shape reconstruction S_q, a manifold representation can be obtained using the kernel function based on S_q and mapping $\mathbb{A}$.

3   Experiments

3.1   Clinical Data

To train the prediction model, a database of baseline 3-D spine reconstructions was used, originating from 133 patients demonstrating several types of deformities. Patients were recruited from a single center prospective study [4], with the inclusion criteria being evaluated by an orthopedic surgeon and a main curvature angle between 11 and 40°. Patients were divided in two groups based on the severity of the main curve, with the first group composed of 52 progressive patients with a difference of 6° between the first and last visits, which varied between 6 and 48 months. The second group was composed of 81 non-progressive (NP) patients with a difference of 6° or less between baseline and longitudinal scans (up to 3 years after baseline). This threshold was selected based on the level of confidence for radiographic measurements.

This cohort was comprised of 116 girls and 17 boys. The mean age of subjects was 12.6 years old at the time of the first visit. The average main Cobb angle on the frontal plane at the first visit was $22.1° \pm 8.4°$. For each patient in the dataset, a 3-D reconstruction of the spine was obtained from the method described in the methodology, from which a series of clinical 2D and 3-D geometrical parameters can be computed, such as computerized Cobb angles and angles of planes of maximum curvature. There were 32 right thoracic curves, 48 double curves (22 main thoracic, and 26 main left lumbar), 7 triple curves, 36 left thoracolumbar curves, and 10 right lumbar or left thoracic curve.

3.2   Automatic Classification Results

In this study, a 9-fold cross-validation was performed to assess the performance of the method. We evaluated the classification accuracy for discriminating between NP and P scoliotic patients using the baseline 3-D reconstructions, by training the model using vertebral shapes, inter-vertebral (IV) poses and with a combination of both shape+IV poses. Figure 2 shows P and NP examples from similar baseline examinations. Figure 3 presents ROC curves obtained by the proposed and comparative methods such as SVM (nonlinear RBF kernel), LLE and LL-LVM [15]. The discriminative nature of the proposed framework clearly shows an improvement to standard learning approaches models which were trained using shape only, IV poses only and combined features. Table 1 presents accuracy, sensitivity and specificity results for classification between NP and P patients. It illustrates that increased accuracy (77.4%) can be achieved by combining shape and IV pose features, showing the benefit of extracting complementary features from the dataset for prediction purposes. When comparing the performance of the proposed method to the other learning methods (SVM, LLE, LL-LVM), the probabilistic model integrating similarity graphs shows a statistically significant improvement ($p < 0.01$) to all three approaches based on paired t-test.

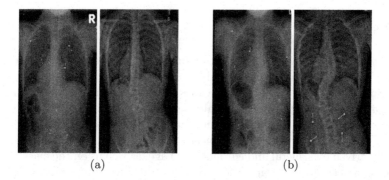

(a)   (b)

Fig. 2. Examples of similar baseline 3D reconstructions with different longitudinal outcomes. (a) A non-progressive case. (b) A progressive case.

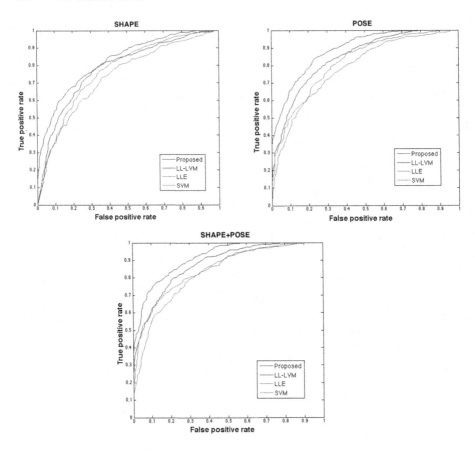

Fig. 3. ROC curves comparing the SVM, LLE and LL-LVM with the proposed method for NP/P prediction using only shape, only inter-vertebral (IV) poses and combining both shape and IV poses.

4   Discussion

With the intent of determining optimal surgical strategies and treatments for patients with AIS, quantification and classification of spinal deformities such as AIS in 3-D remains challenging because of the difficulty of translating complex geometrical concepts into clinically applicable paradigms [16]. A number of studies have investigated into pattern classification based on explicit clinical parameters. It is recognized from clinical experience that progression in AIS is primarily driven by skeletal and chronological age, as well as on the class of deformation (thoracic, lumbar), and the severity of the curve deformation. However these discrete parameters, such as curve magnitude obtained at the first visit are not sufficient to accurately predict whether the main curve will progress or not. Sangole et al. [17] found spinal curves in scoliosis have abnormal orientations in 3-D space with respect to the sagittal plane. The proposed framework is able to

Table 1. Performance results for conversion prediction from between P and NP patients, compared to SVM, LLE and LL-LVM [15]. Training performed using only shape information, only inter-vertebral (IV) poses and combined shape-IV features. AUC = Area under curve.

Data	Method	Accuracy	Sensitivity	Specificity	AUC
Shape	SVM	58.5	53.6	62.7	0.614
	LLE	66.2	63.5	67.1	0.701
	LL-LVM	70.7	72.7	67.9	0.762
	Proposed	**72.6**	**77.8**	**70.0**	**0.769**
Poses	SVM	53.7	48.4	56.7	0.560
	LLE	60.8	59.0	64.7	0.651
	LL-LVM	69.0	70.7	71.6	0.749
	Proposed	**75.0**	**77.5**	**74.3**	**0.794**
Shape+poses	SVM	61.6	54.3	64.1	0.658
	LLE	67.0	66.5	63.3	0.733
	LL-LVM	69.5	76.3	**72.6**	0.783
	Proposed	**78.6**	**85.1**	72.5	**0.827**

process the entire spine model which adds significant insight on the predominant features used for the prediction of curve progression. A previous study by the Scoliosis Research Society 3-D Scoliosis Committee demonstrated that similar 3-D profiles can lead to different 3-D morphology progression and thus stressed on quantifying 3-D deformations. In [4], a number of clinical parameters including the angulation of the main curve and apical inter-vertebral axial rotation are leading predictors. The main problem in dividing the different geometrics of deformation as potential risk factor of progression is the lack of robustness based on the accuracy of these measures. Villemure et al. [18] found a concomitant progression between curve severity and 3-D vertebral body wedging. This observation was also seen in this study as it reveals increased local vertebra deformation from the baseline reconstruction is correlated to the predicted class outcome. Our results also show an increase in performance when using inter-vertebral transformations in comparison to only geometric shape represented by vertex positions of all vertebral models. The combination of both features yield the highest overall accuracy with classification rates over 78%.

The main contribution of this paper consists in describing anatomical variations of the scoliotic spine in a discriminant nonlinear graph embedding with Grassmannian manifolds to detect wether a patient's deformation will progress or not. An accurate modeling of the vertebra shape and the overall pose of the articulated spine model in relation to inter-vertebral transformation enables to capture the inherent geometric properties of spinal deformations. This is critical to construct a reliable training set of geometric spine shapes from various pathological groups. A manifold embedding including intrinsic and penalty graphs measuring similarity within clinical relevant groups and between P and NP patients was trained to differentiate between the different spine shapes which have different progression outcomes. Canonical correlation kernels creates a secondary manifold to simplify the deviation estimation from normality, improving detection of pathology compared to standard LLE. Experiments show the need of nonlinear embedding of the learning data, and the relevance of the proposed method for stratifying different stages of curve progression. In the context of AIS, the method can improve for the early detection of the curve evolution with promising classification rates based on ground-truth knowledge.

The technique presented in this paper provides a means to predict the progression of the spinal deformities in both thoracolumbar and lumbar regions, which is critical to determine the optimal follow-up strategy and determine treatment options. Populations of 3-D scoliotic patients obtained from sparse and shape+pose models can be analyzed and subsequently classified in order to determine patterns in pathological cases. Hence personalized 3-D reconstructions of thoracic/lumbar spines obtained from a cohort of various deformation classes were analyzed with a discriminant manifold algorithm.

5   Conclusion and Future Work

We presented a method for predicting scoliotic curve progression using baseline 3-D reconstructions of spine models generated from biplanar X-ray images. By taking a more global approach for curve progression prediction, using discriminative machine learning algorithms that minimize the effects of noisy data, the proposed methodology yields classification rates that are encouraging for clinical assessment of spinal deformities and personalizing follow-up examinations. This allows for a quantitative analysis of the spinal deformity based on the implicit representation of the entire spine geometry, which is more representative of the nature of deformation. The results of our current study suggest that a more stable estimation of the 3-D progression prediction in scoliosis is within reach. The advantage of using machine learning techniques to classify scoliosis is that it synthesizes knowledge from hundreds of samples with known outcomes. This opens the possibility for a 3-D classification paradigm of scoliosis that will not only be more user friendly, but also more accurate in describing this deformity. Future work will try to predict morphology evolution through spatio-temporal models, which will not only output binary classifications, but also predict structural outcomes.

References

1. Fong, D.Y.T., Lee, C.F., Cheung, K.M.C., Cheng, J.C.Y., Ng, B.K.W., Lam, T.P., Mak, K.H., Yip, P.S.F., Luk, K.D.K.: A meta-analysis of the clinical effectiveness of school scoliosis screening. Spine **35**(10), 1061–1071 (2010)
2. Lonstein, J.E., Carlson, J.: The prediction of curve progression in untreated idiopathic scoliosis during growth. J. Bone Joint Surg. Am. **66**(7), 1061–1071 (1984)

 3. Nault, M.L., Mac-Thiong, J.M., Roy-Beaudry, M., Labelle, H., Parent, S., et al.: Three-dimensional spine parameters can differentiate between progressive and non-progressive patients with AIS at the initial visit: a retrospective analysis. J. Pediatr. Orthop. **33**(6), 618–623 (2013)
 4. Nault, M.L., Mac-Thiong, J.M., Roy-Beaudry, M., Turgeon, I., et al.: Three-dimensional spinal morphology can differentiate between progressive and nonprogressive patients with adolescent idiopathic scoliosis at the initial presentation: a prospective study. Spine **39**(10), E601 (2014)
 5. Duong, L., Cheriet, F., Labelle, H.: Three-dimensional classification of spinal deformities using fuzzy clustering. Spine **31**, 923–30 (2006)
 6. Kadoury, S., Labelle, H.: Classification of three-dimensional thoracic deformities in adolescent idiopathic scoliosis from a multivariate analysis. Eur. Spine J. **21**, 40–49 (2012)
 7. Lawrence, N., Hyvarinen, A.: Probabilistic non-linear principal component analysis with gaussian process latent variable models. JMLR **6**, 1783–1816 (2005)
 8. Kanaujia, A., Sminchisescu, C., Metaxas, D.: Spectral latent variable models for perceptual inference. In: ICCV, pp. 1–8 (2007)
 9. Thong, W., Parent, S., Wu, J., Aubin, C.E., Labelle, H., Kadoury, S.: Three-dimensional morphology study of surgical adolescent idiopathic scoliosis patient from encoded geometric models. Eur. Spine J. **25**(10), 3104–3113 (2016)
10. Harandi, M., Sanderson, C., et al.: Graph embedding discriminant analysis on Grassmannian manifolds for improved image set matching. In: CVPR, p. 2705 (2011)
11. Korez, R., Aubert, B., Cresson, T., Parent, S., de Guise, J., Kadoury, S., et al.: Sparse and multi-object pose+shape modeling of the three-dimensional scoliotic spine. In: IEEE 13th International Symposium on Biomedical Imaging (ISBI), pp. 225–228. IEEE (2016)
12. Bossa, M., Olmos, S.: Multi-object statistical pose+shape models. In: 4th IEEE International Symposium on Biomedical Imaging: From Nano to Macro, pp. 1204–1207. IEEE (2007)
13. Kadoury, S., Cheriet, F., Labelle, H.: Personalized X-ray 3D reconstruction of the scoliotic spine from statistical and image-based models. IEEE Trans. Med. Imag. **28**, 1422–1435 (2009)
14. Roweis, S., Saul, L.: Nonlinear dimensionality reduction by locally linear embedding. Science **290**, 2323–2326 (2000)
15. Park, M., Jitkrittum, W., Qamar, A., Szabó, Z., Buesing, L., Sahani, M.: Bayesian manifold learning: the locally linear latent variable model (LL-LVM). In: Advances in Neural Information Processing Systems, pp. 154–162 (2015)
16. Kadoury, S., Shen, J., Parent, S.: Global geometric torsion estimation in adolescent idiopathic scoliosis. Med. Biol. Eng. Comput. **52**(4), 309–319 (2014)
17. Sangole, A., Aubin, C., Labelle, H., et al.: Three-dimensional classification of thoracic scoliotic curves. Spine **34**, 91–99 (2009)
18. Villemure, I., Aubin, C., Grimard, G., Dansereau, J., Labelle, H.: Progression of vertebral and spinal three-dimensional deformities in adolescent idiopathic scoliosis: a longitudinal study. Spine **26**(20), 2244–2250 (2001)

Author Index

Printed in the United States
By Bookmasters